The Birdkeepers' Guides
Parrotlets

Nikki Moustaki

Parrotlets

Project Team
Editor: Tom Mazorlig
Indexer: Elizabeth Walker
Design: Mary Ann Kahn

TFH Publications®
President/CEO: Glen S. Axelrod
Executive Vice President: Mark E. Johnson
Publisher: Christopher T. Reggio
Production Manager: Kathy Bontz

TFH Publications, Inc.®
One TFH Plaza
Third and Union Avenues
Neptune City, NJ 07753

Printed and bound in China
12 13 14 15 16 1 3 5 7 9 8 6 4 2

Library of Congress Cataloging-in-Publication Data
Moustaki, Nikki, 1970-.
  Parrotlets / Nikki Moustaki.
     p. cm.
  Includes index.
  ISBN 978-0-7938-1481-7 (alk. paper)
  1. Parrotlets. I. Title.
  SF473.P3M675 2012
  636.6'865--dc23
                        2012003382

The Leader in Responsible Animal Care for Over 50 Years!®
www.tfh.com

Contents

Introducing Parrotlets

They are tiny, feisty, affectionate, and mischievous. No, not toddlers–parrotlets! These "pocket parrots" are relatively new to bird circles, but they have caught on fast. Their personality is fearless and lively, and they pack a lot of intelligence and energy into a little body. Most are about the size of a budgie, but shorter and stouter, almost like a tiny Amazon parrot.

There are seven species of parrotlets and several dozen subspecies. They originate in Central and South America, Mexico, and some Caribbean islands. Parrotlets have been known to Europeans since the 1700s and are growing in popularity every year as more people discover the "big bird in the little bird's body."

Your parrotlet is probably not from the wilds of the rainforest, however. A bird breeder who took a particular interest in parrotlets hatched your bird and handfed it so that it would be tame. Even though parrots are still considered wild–not domestic–your parrotlet was "born" (hatched) in captivity. Parrotlets are said to have a lifespan of over 20 years, but no one is positive of this, because they haven't

Male Pacific parrotlets have blue coloration on the wings, rump, and face, while the females are mostly different shades of green.

In the Wild

The wild parrotlet is an active bird whose days are filled with flying, foraging for food, playing, keeping away from predators, finding nesting sites and nesting, protecting the nest, and raising young. The wild parrotlet feeds primarily on grass seeds but will also eat fruit and fruit seeds as well. The average clutch (number of babies) is five to six. In captivity, your companion parrotlet does not have much to do. Because of the lack of real exercise, companion parrotlets are prone to become overweight, which can lead to fatty tumors and a greatly reduced lifespan. To help your parrotlet remain fit and trim, provide him with as much exercise as possible.

been kept regularly in captivity for very long. Perhaps they can live even longer with ideal care.

When I got my first pair of breeding parrotlets in 1993 they were a relative rarity and color mutations were just emerging. I knew only a handful of other bird-keepers that fancied them, and they were very expensive. Today there are parrotlet societies and clubs dedicated to these robust little birds, and they have come down in price a little. I'm happy that they have become so popular because they make great companions at a fraction of the noise made by other parrots and the space and budget devoted to them.

The Species of Parrotlets

The word "parrotlet" basically means "little parrot." The seven species occur in a single genus called *Forpus*. They seem to be closely related to the Amazon parrots and the pionus parrots (genera *Amazona* and *Pionus* respectively), but parrotlets are much smaller than those two groups.

Sometimes information on parrotlets is bundled with information about other diminutive parrots, such as *Brotogeris* and *Touit*, but this book will focus on the *Forpus* parrotlets, which are the seven species that most bird keepers in the United States refer to when they say "parrotlets."

The Pacific Parrotlet (aka the Celestial Parrotlet)

The Pacific parrotlet (*Forpus coelestis*) is fast becoming one of the most popular small birds in the country, and it is the most common of the seven parrotlet species. Originating in Mexico and Central and South America, Pacific parrotlets are prized for their diminutive size (about 5 inches [13 cm] long) and their "big" personalities.

Pacifics are dimorphic, meaning that there is a visible difference in appearance between the sexes, the coloration of males and females in this species being a case in point. Males are green with blue on the rump, part of the wings, and a blue streak on the face, while females are mainly different shades of green. Some recent color mutations have been developed, including blue, white, yellow, pied, and darker green, among others.

Pacific parrotlets are not noisy birds, making them great apartment pets. They will repeat words and simple phrases but are not known to be the finest talkers of the parrotlet group. If you want a great pet, it is best to keep only one bird, as a pair of parrotlets may bond closely to each other, to the possible exclusion of the owner. If you do want a pair and want them to maintain their pet quality, you must handle both of them every single day.

Pacifics are very spirited and can become aggressive if left for too long without handling. Even though they are tiny, do not underestimate that strong beak.

You will probably acquire your Pacific parrotlet as a hand-raised youngster, and more than likely it will be from a breeder. Most general pet shops do not carry them, although this is changing as parrotlets grow in popularity. Bird-specific shops should have a good selection of parrotlets. I got my first Pacific parrotlets from a breeder, and I bought a pair, hoping to breed them so that I could hand-raise a baby for myself. Well, they

Wild blue-winged parrotlet feeding on fruit in northern Argentina.

went to nest, and to my surprise their eggs looked like a physical impossibility—they seemed as big as the hen herself, certainly larger than my lovebirds' eggs!

Pacific parrotlets can live for 20 to 25 years or more if cared for properly, with a nutritious diet and plenty of exercise. They will live well in a cockatiel-sized cage or larger, but make sure that the bars are not spaced too wide, or they might get their little heads caught and become injured. They enjoy lots of toys, including rope to unravel (make sure to trim rope toys regularly) and soft wood to destroy. Their beaks are formidable for such small birds, and they love to chew, so watch them closely around wooden furniture.

A Pacific may look like a simple green parakeet, but it is not priced like one. As with many other bird species, these birds will probably go down in price as breeders fill the market with them, though some mutations may always fetch a high price. If you want a feisty little clown that is capable

Green-rumped parrotlets tend to be gentler than Pacifics and may take longer to settle in to new surroundings.

of a strong human/bird bond and of mimicking speech, the Pacific parrotlet may be the perfect bird for you.

Green-Rumped Parrotlet

The next most popular species is the green-rumped parrotlet (*Forpus*

Parrotlet IQ

The parrotlet is a highly intelligent little bird, able to recognize the people and things in his life. Each one is an individual with his own tastes and personality. Parrotlets aren't known as the best talkers in the parrot world, but some can amass a few dozen words and phrases. Overall, they are affectionate companions that bond readily to humans who can pay regular attention to them. A parrotlet that is left too long without attention can "revert" to more feisty behavior. Some individuals are even smart enough to try to "rule" the house with an iron wing, which is fairly humorous considering this bird's size.

Leg Bands

Most states require breeders selling birds to put a "closed band" on one of the bird's legs before it can be sold. Engraved into it are the initials of the breeder, the state where the bird was bred, the year the bird was hatched, and a number that is unique to your individual bird. This last number helps the breeder keep records of the babies. Some people have this band removed, especially if it is irritating the bird or there is a chance that the band will become caught on something in the cage or aviary, causing the leg to break or the skin to tear. Do not *ever* try to remove this band yourself. Your avian veterinarian or local bird shop has a special tool to remove it. If you try to remove it yourself you will break or injure your bird's leg.

passerinus). Like the Pacific, the males have blue on the wings and the females do not. They are a little gentler than the Pacific parrotlet but may take a longer time to acclimate to new surroundings. This species might be better for the parrotlet novice, or someone who may have "beak fear." They are just slightly smaller than the Pacific parrotlet and truly look like a diminutive Amazon parrot. Because of their gentler nature, this may be a better species for a child's pet than a Pacific. Their lifespan is over 20 years with the proper care.

An interesting green-rumped fact: in 1990, Trinidad and Tobago put a beautiful graphic of a pair of these birds on a postage stamp! Very fitting for this tiny parrotlet species, which is found on several Caribbean islands.

Blue-Winged Parrotlet

The blue-winged parrotlet (*Forpus*

xanthopterygius) is also a dimorphic species, the male having blue on his wings and rump and the female being all green. This species is often confused with the green-rumped parrotlet because they look very similar. They are approximately 5 ½ inches (14 cm) in length, similar in size to the green-rumped. They are not as readily available in captivity as the Pacific but can be found if you research them a bit. As for personality, they are similar to the green-rumped in that they are a bit gentler and shyer than the Pacific.

Mexican Parrotlet

The Mexican parrotlet (*Forpus cyanopygius*) is found in Mexico (hence the name) and is slightly heavier and stouter than the more common species. Mexican parrotlets are sexually dimorphic like the other parrotlets, with the male having blue (turquoise) on the wings and rumps and the female lacking this color. It is unlikely that you will find the Mexican parrotlet readily for sale. This species is in danger of becoming extinct in the wild and is difficult to breed in captivity. Most of the captive Mexican parrotlets are in breeding programs. When handfed, the Mexican parrotlet is a gentle companion. Hopefully breeding programs will boost their numbers.

Spectacled Parrotlet

The tiny spectacled parrotlet (*Forpus conspicillatus*) is an up-and-coming species to watch. There aren't many of them in captivity, but breeders are paying particular attention to them and numbers are on the rise. The spectacled is the smallest of the parrotlets and the most brilliantly colored. It is called the "spectacled" because the male has a blue ring around each eye, giving the appearance of wearing a pair of glasses. Females have a brilliant green eye ring. Their personality is sweet, and they are as clown-like as the other parrotlet species, with a nature similar to that of the green-rumped.

Yellow-Faced Parrotlet

The yellow-faced parrotlet (*Forpus xanthops*) is the largest of the seven parrotlet species at approximately 6

The spectacled parrotlet is still rare in aviculture but is becoming more common.

Small Bird, Little Noise

The size of the parrot usually determines the loudness of its voice. The parrotlet is chatty, but it's not loud, making it a great bird for apartment dwellers. However, the more parrotlets you have the noisier they will be, so keep that in mind. They also tend to be most chatty at dawn and dusk.

inches (15 cm) in length. It is nearly as rare as the Mexican parrotlet in the wild and isn't found in captivity except in breeding programs intended to increase its numbers. There are said to be fewer than 100 individuals in the United States. Don't expect to find one at your local pet store.

Dusky-Billed Parrotlet

The dusky-billed parrotlet, also known as Sclater's parrotlet (*Forpus sclateri*), is very rare, and since it has not been imported into the United States it has never been bred here and is therefore unavailable. It is originally found in the South American rainforests in the Amazon River Basin to the foothills of the Andes.

Physical Characteristics

Parrotlets are roughly 5 inches (13 cm) long and weigh in at about an ounce, give or take a few grams. They occur in several color mutations and patterns, with more being developed each year. You will probably easily find only about five or six distinct colors/patterns at your local breeder, and even fewer at the pet store. There is no difference in the companionability among the different colors.

In the wild, parrotlets come in only one color, green, the "nominate" or normal color. The other colors, the mutations, are naturally occurring deviations from the normal color. A wild parrotlet that was any color other than green would be an easy mark for a predator, and probably would not live long enough to pass along his genes. In captivity, breeders single out these mutations and breed them widely so that new ones can develop.

Parrotlets are feisty birds, often referred to as big parrots in small bodies.

Hand-Fed Babies

Most parrotlet breeders hand feed the babies they want to sell. This means that the breeder will take the baby away from the parents when it is still reliant on them and take over their parental duties, usually at about ten days of age. By the time a parrotlet reaches a pet shop and stays there a while before it is sold, it may lose some of its companionability—this happens fairly quickly in parrotlets, especially where there are other parrotlets around to play with. Try to get yours from a breeder or get one that has had some hands-on time with pet store employees.

All parrotlets, with the exception of some of the rarer mutations, are sexually dimorphic, which means that it's easy to visually tell the difference between the sexes. In most cases the male has blue markings on the wings, rump, or near the eyes (or another color in some of the color mutations) and the female does not. Immature birds look similar to females.

Beyond color, the parrotlet's body also has several fascinating elements:

Eyes: A parrotlet's eyes should be round, clear, and bright. There should be no crust or discharge from the eyes. They should show an attitude of alertness.

Nares and Cere: A parrotlet's nostrils are called nares, and they are located on the cere, which is just above the beak. The nares should be clean and without discharge.

Ears: The parrotlet's ears are located just behind the eye toward the back of the head. The ear is covered by fine feathers and looks like a hole in the bird's head. It is not visible in a healthy adult unless he's wet from bathing. The ear may be visible in an ill bird that is not well-groomed or is losing feathers.

Feathers: A healthy parrotlet's feathers are shiny and tight, and they lie flat against the body. A parrotlet with ruffled feathers may be ill or temporarily cold. A parrotlet with bald patches is either ill, plucking his own feathers, or being plucked by a cagemate.

Feet: A parrotlet's feet should be free of debris and nimble enough to perch and climb. Sometimes a parrotlet becomes crippled in the nest as a baby and has splayed legs or other foot problems, but can still make a great companion.

Vent: The vent is beneath the bird at the base of the tail; it is the place from where waste is eliminated and eggs are laid. The vent area should be clean, not crusted with feces or other material.

Temperament and Behavior

Young parrotlets are docile and easily tamed, but they won't stay that way

Parrotlet Color Mutations

Though color mutations in birds are a natural occurrence, selective breeding encourages and enhances the production of more color mutations than would occur in the wild. The word "mutation" isn't a phrase out of a science-fiction movie when it applies to birds. When bird-keepers use the term "color mutation," it simply means that a part of the bird's genetic makeup has naturally altered slightly to create a physical change in the bird's appearance. When bird-keepers breed these color mutations together, the result is a continuation of the mutation. The result in Pacific parrotlets is a variety of colors, including:

- Blue (dark eyes)
- American yellow (dark eyes, also known as dilute)
- Fallow (light yellowish green with red eyes)
- Fallow blue (red eyes, blue markings)
- Fallow yellow (yellow/blue markings with red eyes)
- Lutino (yellow with red eyes, males have white markings instead of blue)
- Albino (white with red eyes, sex can not be determined visually)
- American white (light blue/white with dark eyes)
- Cinnamon (light yellowish gray, also known as Isabel)
- Pied (splotchy markings in a variety of colors)
- Yellow head (blue with a yellow face)

unless they are handled regularly. They can be aggressive and bossy birds. Fortunately, the parrotlet's beak isn't large, so the bite isn't terrible, but it can hurt. However, even adult parrotlets can be tamed with a little time and a lot of patience. In general they are loyal and affectionate to their human companions, though they may wander off in search of something good to chew (and probably something inappropriate!). Females can become strong-willed and crabby (read: mean) when they're protecting eggs. They can lay eggs even when a male is not present. Males may make more docile companions.

A healthy parrotlet is active and vocal. Much of his noise sounds like chitter-chatter, and at times like screeching, but it's not loud. A fit and happy parrotlet will be quite noisy; a silent bird might actually be ill, especially if his cagemates are chirping up a storm. Parrotlets even chitter-chatter in their sleep during a daytime nap, but they won't make a peep at night when the lights are out. Some people like the chatter and others are driven crazy by the persistence of it. In general, parrotlet voices are pleasant.

Wild parrotlets vocalize insistently around dawn and at dusk, and then chirp pretty much all day long as they go about their business of finding food and courting. Your companion parrotlet will do the same, with the occasional break for a catnap. You will not get him to stop vocalizing, but you can choose the time that he begins his daily routine by using a dark cage cover. However, if your parrotlet is already used to vocalizing at a certain time of day, it's unlikely that a cover will help. Birds have a very good internal clock and can tell when it's time to wake up. If you do use a cage cover, make sure that you wash it with a scent-free detergent and that you dry it without a scented dryer sheet, as these things can irritate your bird's respiratory system.

As for basic behavior, parrotlets are generally active and perky and can even be quite bossy. A bird sitting on the bottom of the cage, fluffed and sleepy, might be ill or injured. Healthy parrotlets are generally wandering around the cage socializing, eating, and bathing. The one in the corner on the bottom of the cage is trying to take a "time out" and get away from the others because he doesn't feel well or is being picked on.

Most birds like to perch in the

Daily Care

- Offering fresh water twice daily.
- Offering and changing fresh foods daily.
- Conducting safe playtime out of the cage daily.
- Watching for signs of illness and taking your parrotlet to the veterinarian if you suspect something is wrong or in the event of an accident.
- Parrotlet-proofing your home.
- Watching other pets closely when the bird is out of his cage.
- Making sure that the cage is out of drafts and that the bird's environment doesn't get too cold or too warm.
- Checking the cage and toys daily for signs of dangerous wear and tear.

Talk-ability

Not all parrotlets will talk, but some individuals do learn a few words and phrases. There's no real way to choose a parrotlet that will talk for certain, but some bird-keepers say to watch a group of young birds to see which one is the chattiest. That may be the one that will talk. It's not fool-proof, but it's worth a shot!

highest spot possible, because a high place makes a secure lookout point. Birds are prey animals and are always on the lookout for predators. You may find that your parrotlet stops vocalizing when your dog or cat enters the room, or becomes agitated when it sees a hawk overhead, even if there's a window between the predator and your bird.

Being in a high spot isn't the only behavioral instinct that your companion parrotlet will exhibit. Even a single bird has the natural instinct to breed and will try to do so with a toy, a coop cup, or his owner's hand. A parrotlet that is stimulated to breed may also become cranky and nippy. In the wild, parrotlets breed when there's an abundance of light, food, and water, which is most of the year for this tropical bird (with the exception of the Mexican parrotlet, which has a particular breeding season). Your parrotlet has the same programming. If he does not give up his breeding behavior, cut down the amount of light he receives to about nine or ten hours a day, serve water in a smaller cup (to discourage bathing for a short time), and remove the toy or cup that your parrotlet believes is his mate. When the clocks change in the fall, you can go back to bathing your bird, and his or her behavior should return to normal. Or, better yet, get your parrotlet a companion to alleviate the frustration of not having a friend.

Perch Mates

Males and females make equally good companions depending on the individual. Companionability has much less to do with sex than it does with handling and socialization. Handfed parrotlets are very friendly, especially if the guardian takes the time to keep handling the bird. If left alone for too long, a single parrotlet can lose some of its companionability. If you can't pay much attention to your parrotlet, consider getting him or her a birdy companion—*only* another parrotlet—do not try to mix this bird with any non-parrotlet species or you may come home to find that one of your birds has flown to heaven, to put it nicely. You can mix species of parrotlets together, but you must make sure they won't breed, creating hybrids. If you keep different species together, keep only all-male or all-female groups.

The Pacific parrotlet is the most popular pet species and is available in several color mutations.

Life Span

A parrotlet can live to be 20 to 25 years old, but these are just estimates – parrotlets have not been kept in captivity for long enough to really know how long they live with the proper care. It is known that female breeding parrotlets have a shorter lifespan than non-breeders, as do those hens that lay eggs constantly (with or without a mate).

There are only two reliable ways to tell the age of your parrotlet. The first is immature coloring – juvenile birds look similar to females but will develop their mature colors after their first feather molt. However, in most parrotlets the blue markings that indicate the male sex are there in the first feathering and get deeper after the first molt. The second way to tell a bird's age is a closed leg band, which is generally put on the leg by the breeder when the parrotlet is a hatchling (two or three days old), and it is engraved with the breeder's initials, state, and the month and year in which the bird was hatched.

2

Parrotlet Supplies

Part of the fun of getting a parrotlet is the shopping you get to do for your new best friend. Because the parakeet (or budgie) is so popular there are hundreds, perhaps thousands, of different toys and accessories you can use for your parrotlet because he is of the same relative size. However, your parrotlet's beak is a bit more powerful than that of a parakeet, more like that of a lovebird, so keep that in mind when choosing accessories—you want to choose items that are well made and not easily broken.

Bigger Is Better

A parrotlet's cage should be as large and roomy as possible. It should be big enough to accommodate perches, food dishes, and toys while still allowing your bird some space for flying. Remember to always check bar widths in larger cages. Your parrotlet is small and can easily stick his head or entire body through widely spaced bars.

Most cages made for cockatiels will work well for housing parrotlets.

Housing

There are dozens of parrotlet housing options at any pet shop or e-commerce retailer. But which one is right for your bird? The housing decision might appear easy to make because it involves very basic considerations. For example, perhaps you want a certain color, or you have budget restrictions. Though those things can influence your decision, they should not be the sole deciding factors in buying a cage. Remember, your parrotlet will be spending considerable time in his new home. A cage should be your parrotlet's home, not his prison, so you want the largest cage possible.

Square or rectangular cages are a better choice than round ones. Your parrotlet will like a corner to scrunch into, and a round cage does not offer that option. Also, some round cages have bars that taper toward the top, which can be a choking hazard should the bird get his neck caught between the bars. Tapered bars can also catch a nail and cause it or the toe to break.

Some people choose not to have a cage at all, believing that the bird will live in the house or in a certain room. This might sound perfect in theory, but it's simply not practical or safe to have your tiny parrotlet flying around the house 24 hours a day. He needs a place to rest, eat, play, and be safe. It's true that birds don't really belong in cages, but for the companion parrotlet the average home presents a great deal of hazards that can be avoided by providing him with his own safe haven.

Cage Size

Avoid cages labeled for parakeets, usually small pastel-colored enclosures that are geared toward the décor of a child's room. They are unacceptable homes for your parrotlet. Instead, choose one that's labeled "flight cage" or "cockatiel cage." In a perfect world, the very minimum size would be 36 inches (91.4 cm) wide x 24 inches (61

Flying Right

Flying is wonderful exercise, perfectly suited for birds, but it's not always advisable to have a parrotlet flying inside the average home. With his wing feathers clipped, he can get exercise from flapping, playing with toys, climbing ropes and ladders, and plenty of playtime out of the cage with his owners; however, flying is ideal. Walking around on the floor might seem like good exercise, but there's a risk that your parrotlet can be stepped on (especially if your carpet and your parrotlet are similar in color), or could become a snack for the family dog or cat. However, keeping a parrotlet flighted in a large aviary is ideal—just make sure that you don't take him outside or provide him with any opportunity to escape into the great blue yonder.

Safety vs. Design

The best materials for a parrotlet cage are safe metals and hard plastics. Wooden and antique cages can be dangerous because they are easily destroyed and may harbor bacteria or contain toxins. Buy a cage that will be comfortable for your bird rather than one that appeals to you because of its design or because it suits your décor.

cm) deep x 48 inches (121.9 cm) tall. Buy a cage even larger than that if you can.

Even though a cage is nice and roomy, it may not be safe for a parrotlet. Make sure that the bars are not wide enough for the bird to stick his head through, which can cause him to panic and injure himself, perhaps fatally. The bar spacing should be no more than ½ to 5/8 inch (1.27 to 1.59 cm). There are a lot of larger flight or aviary cages on the market that will be perfect for your parrotlet.

Cage Materials

When shopping for cages, think about practicality, comfort, and safety features first. The cosmetics of the cage should be secondary. A pretty cage is not always the best or safest home for your parrotlet. Fortunately, manufacturers have gotten savvy in the past few years and are designing more attractive cages with both décor and safety in mind.

Powder-Coated

Most cages are made of metal and plastic, and some are coated with paint to add color and texture. Powder-coated cages are made by spraying the bars with a specific type of powdered paint and then using high temperatures to melt it onto the metal. This is a very sturdy and safe type of paint that resists chipping. Make sure that the coating on the bars is nontoxic and won't harm your bird. If you notice that your parrotlet is picking away at the coating, *remove the bird from the cage immediately* and get a new cage that does not have a coating. Ingestion of paint or plastic coating can be deadly.

Make sure that the bars of your parrotlet's cage are spaced correctly. He must not be able to get his head stuck between the bars.

Your bird will feel most secure if his cage is placed in a corner.

a nice feature for allergy sufferers. You will have to clean an acrylic cage frequently to make sure that no moisture builds up in the tray. Some new models on the market include a solid front or sides that help keep your floors clean.

Others

Some decorative metal cages have scrollwork that can catch a toe and cause it to break or bleed, which is dangerous for a little bird. Look for simplicity in design and leave the decorative cages to wooden birds. Likewise, wooden pagoda-style cages are unacceptable for parrotlets because they can easily chew their way out of them. Stick with safe metals and plastics.

Stainless Steel

Stainless steel cages are a great option because they are nontoxic and you won't have to worry about paint chipping. They are an expensive option, but they don't rust and should last the life of your bird.

Acrylic

Acrylic cages are expensive, but they eliminate mess. They are attractive, safe, and save you time on cleaning the area around the cage. Some even come with mechanical ventilation that clears the air inside the cage,

Cage Doors

Look for a cage with a door that opens on one side with hinges, like the door to a house, or one that opens from the top and pulls down. Guillotine-style doors are popular in the less expensive cages, but they are dangerous because they can snap down on a parrotlet's head or neck. If you already have a cage with guillotine-style doors, buy some stainless steel quick links online or from your hardware store and keep those doors locked shut. Spring clips will work as well, but if your bird is determined enough he can move the spring mechanism with his beak and get caught in it.

Where to Place the Cage

Once you've gotten a cage, situate it in your home in a spot that gets some traffic, an area that maintains a sense of relative calm but is well-attended by family members. For example, the living room, family room, and TV room are all good choices, but a

Keep your parrotlet in a living room or family room where he can interact with his human flock.

hallway is not. Don't put the bird in a room that won't get enough traffic, like a child's room, bedroom, den, or back room, because your parrotlet needs a lot of attention and is likely to feel he's missing his "flock" if relegated to an out-of-the-way place. Avoid placing the cage in rooms that may contain fumes or have temperature changes, like the bathroom, kitchen, or garage.

Once you've decided on a location, choose a corner of the room to place the cage in. Ideally, it should be near a window, but not against it. Activities outside may frighten the bird, so he should have a safe spot in the cage near the wall to retreat to—there may be animals outside that scare him, passing cars, or other disturbances. Don't hang the cage in the middle of the room or place it out in the open. It should be against at least one wall for the bird to feel secure. Make sure that the spot isn't drafty and doesn't get too much direct sunlight.

The cage should be high enough so that the family cat or dog can't easily get to it. Birds prefer high locations and will feel very insecure on the ground. Parrotlets are canopy and mid-level brush feeders in the wild, preferring to be higher than ground level. You don't want your parrotlet to live in a constant state of fear. He will have a better vantage point the higher he is, which will make him feel safer and happier.

Cage Alternatives

It's absurd to call any bird a "cage

Bird-Proofing

If your bird is going to spend any time outside his cage, you will need to carefully bird-proof your home. Here's a list of things to cover:

- Ceiling fans: Remove fans or put tape over the switch that turns them on.

- Electrical cords: Wrap up all cords and hide them.

- Fly paper: Don't use it.

- Fumes: Eliminate nonstick cookware from your home (the fumes from heated nonstick cookware can kill birds); eliminate aerosol cans, scented candles, and all air fresheners.

- Halogen lamps: These become very hot and can burn and kill a parrotlet that lands on one.

- Household cleaners: Put away all cleaners, fertilizers, jewelry cleaners, paints, and glues.

- Laundry and bedding: Always make sure that your parrotlet is accounted for before doing a load of laundry. Birds can get into the washer, dryer, laundry basket, or in between blankets and sheets.

- Lead: Move stained glass away from the bird's area and put away lead fishing sinkers (and the hooks, of course).

- Smoke: Ban smoking in your home. Nicotine residue builds up on feathers and can cause health disorders.

- Standing water: Cover all standing water, including fish tanks, dog bowls, toilets, pools, fountains, sinks, and pots in the kitchen.

- Windows: Make sure that all windows have screens that don't have any holes in them.

bird," but that's still how companion birds are labeled today. They aren't meant to be in cages, a topic often missed in discussions about bird keeping. There's little consideration about what birds need to do most: fly. An aviary is a large cage that offers ample room for flight and can house several pairs of parrotlets, but always make sure that they are getting along. You can order a small aviary online or buy one from a bird shop. Ideally, it should be large enough to fit a human adult inside comfortably.

A habitat is an aviary taken to the next level. It is larger and contains natural elements, such as plants and running water. Some zoos have

Parrotlet Pastimes

Like most people, you have to come up with ways to keep your parrotlet entertained while you're away from home. Leave the television or the radio on for the bird. A silent environment is stressful for birds, as silence in the wild means that there's a predator nearby. If you can have two or more parrotlets, they can entertain themselves and "talk" to each other, even if they aren't in the same cage. A parrotlet may be entertained by the presence of finches or a canary nearby—not in the same housing. A nearby fish tank or bowl also works, but make sure it's properly covered while the bird is out of the cage to avoid a drowning hazard. Toys are the ultimate entertainment, so be sure to offer several types and rotate them in and out of the cage weekly. Finally, food is very entertaining, so offer a wide variety, especially ones that the bird can play with, like greens woven in-between the bars of the cage, corn on the cob, and air-popped popcorn.

habitats, and they are becoming popular with bird fanciers as well. The idea is to recreate, as closely as possible, the animal's natural environment. Allowing your birds to fly and interact with the sun and the weather is a good start. Since most habitats are built outdoors, there are considerations such as predators and foul weather to contend with, but a well-built and well-planned habitat can withstand such challenges.

Cups and Bowls

The cage you purchased probably came with a couple of cups for seed and water, which are the basics, but you'll need a few more to complete your set. The ones that came with your cage are most likely plastic, which is not the finest material for a coop cup. Plastic can become scratched and harbor bacteria in the grooves of scratches, no matter how well you clean. Stainless steel is a great material for bird cups. It's durable, easy to clean, and might even outlast your bird. Ceramic cups are also a good choice, but the surface can become cracked and crazed (a network of fine cracks making the ceramic look old), and the cup will need to be replaced eventually. Both of these types can be purchased with holders that keep them securely attached to the cage bars. Some parrotlets may not like eating from covered dishes, so keep an eye on your bird if you try them.

Ideally, you will have two complete sets of dishes: two for seed/pellets, two for water, and two for fresh foods. Each day you can remove the dirty dishes and replace them with the clean ones, allowing you to then disinfect and dry the other dishes for the next day. Cleaning stainless steel cups is easy. Wash them every day in warm soapy water, making sure to wipe every surface with a textured sponge, and then rinse well. Once a week, soak the dishes for ten minutes or so in a 10 percent bleach solution (90 percent water) to thoroughly disinfect them.

Tube-style waterers are popular among owners of small birds because the water often stays cleaner longer in the tube—there is less area for the parrotlet to toss food and droppings into. However, just because the water lasts longer doesn't mean that you don't have to change it every day. You also have to disinfect it more often because most tube waterers are made of plastic. Some people also use water bottles. This is risky because the metal tube can lose suction, leaving your bird without water. Also, bacteria grow rapidly inside the metal tube if it's not cleaned properly. Some people advocate using water bottles because bacteria actually grow slower inside

Parrolets enjoy toys of all kinds, including those with paper they can shred.

Parrotlets seem to enjoy swings of all types.

the glass bottle; however, you still have to change the water twice a day, as you would with regular coop cups. I recommend staying away from both tube-waterers and water bottles and stick with regular coop cups.

Beware of tube-style feeders. Because parrotlets hull their seeds rather than eat them whole, it may look as if they are getting plenty of seed when in reality they only have access to the empty hulls. Add fresh seed to the entire tube every day.

Toys

Toys are essential to the health and well being of a single parrotlet. A pair of parrotlets can get along fairly well without many toys, but there's no reason why they shouldn't have a bunch. Toys keep your parrotlet occupied; they give him something to do with an otherwise dull daily life inside a cage. Wild parrotlets work all day at finding food and water and at staying safe. Your parrotlet doesn't get nearly this much exercise, though he does require it. Toys are for chewing, flinging, preening, and carrying out elaborate arguments. A beloved toy can offer a lonely parrotlet a sense of comfort and a feeling of security and home.

Parrotlets love shiny interactive toys that they can fling around or slather with affection. Some toys are directed toward alleviating loneliness, such as mirror toys and floss and preening toys. Though mirror toys are fun and interactive, your parrotlet may become so enamored with his reflection that he becomes obsessed with it. If you notice that your bird is becoming extremely affectionate with his mirror, you might want to remove the mirror temporarily until the bird's affections return to you. However, if this bird doesn't come out of his cage and he gets a lot of joy from playing with the mirror toy, there's nothing wrong with leaving it in his cage permanently.

Parrotlets are destructive and have a powerful beak for their size, which is why some plastic toys geared for parakeets and cockatiels may not be appropriate. If a toy's label says that it's OK for lovebirds, it's probably fine for parrotlets as well. Consider these types of toys:

• Acrylic: These toys are more expensive, but many are fanciful and inventive, well worth the cost.
• Activity centers: These are all-in-one stations that have a lot of different activities, like rotating wheels or pushing beads on a wire.
• Dispensing toys: These toys are containers that dispense food and treats, for example, sunflower seeds. The bird has to work to figure out

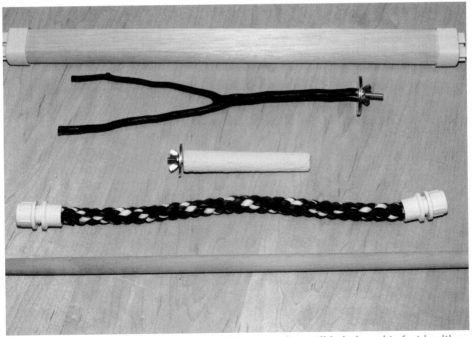

Providing your parrotlet with a variety of different perches will help keep his feet healthy.

Buyer Beware

There are a few popular products on the market that can actually be harmful or deadly for your parrotlet. Spiral millet holders pose a hanging hazard, so steer clear of them. Mite protectors are another risky product. They look like round tins with holes punched on one side. This product contains an insecticide that can be harmful for your bird. Even though parrotlets can get mites, it's unlikely that yours will. Mite protectors are not a substitute for good care and veterinary attention. Cloth huts and stuffed toys are popular these days, but they have been known to cause many deaths by choking and crop impaction.

how to get the seeds out.

- Foot toys: These are stand-alone toys (not attached anywhere on the cage) that your parrotlet can toss around, for example, cylindrical toys with plastic beads inside.
- Foraging toys: These toys have areas where you can hide treats and other goodies (like sisal knots and plastic beads); your bird has to "work" the toy to get the reward.
- Lava and rawhide: These materials are often included with wooden or plastic toys strung on a chain. Both offer the parrotlet a way to keep the beak trim.
- Plastic toys: Some plastic toys are made to withstand the punishment of parrotlets–these are acceptable for your little bird. Plastic indicated for budgies, lovebirds, and cockatiels should be fine.
- Rope: Rope toys are fun to preen and chew, but be sure to trim any loose strings that can easily get caught around a neck or a foot.
- Spooling toys: Some toys include a place to add a roll of calculator paper or toilet paper so that your bird can unravel it and chew to his heart's content. Parrotlets love these spooling toys!
- Swings: Parrotlets love swings, so offer at least one or two. Swings with innovative perches or toys attached are especially useful.
- Wooden toys: Parrotlets love to chew, and toys made from soft wood are perfect for that.

Rotating the toys in and out of the cage on a weekly basis is a good way to keep your parrotlet interested. Removing and replacing them with others also gives you an opportunity to disinfect old toys and refresh any parts that may have frayed or broken. You will need to have an abundance of them on hand to rotate, but be sure to leave the one or two toys that the bird loves inside the cage at all times. If your bird has an absolutely favorite toy, don't remove it–why stress out your bird?

Not all toys sold in the pet shop are safe for your parrotlet. Remember, he has a very tiny head that can get caught in a ring, or he can catch his toes in little places, such as the slots in a jingle bell. Old toys with sharp corners or fraying rope can be dangerous as well. File sharp corners with a nail file and trim any loose strings that could potentially get wrapped around a neck or a foot.

Homemade Toys

Homemade bird toys are usually inventive and interesting and can be fun to make for your parrotlet buddy. Here are a few easy ones to try:

For a homemade foraging toy, wrap millet inside white tissue paper and tie it at the ends with a small length of sisal twine. Hang it or place it in the cage. You might have to tear the paper a little the first time to show the bird what's inside.

For a portable swing, wrap a wooden clothes hanger (one with a pants bar at the bottom) all over with sisal twine. Using lengths of twine, tie plastic buttons, scrunched up tissue paper, and pieces of millet spray to it. You can hang it anywhere you want your parrotlet to hang out with you.

For an activity box/bowl, use a shallow dish filled with different sized marbles, blueberries, cranberries, and air-popped popcorn; the bird can move all of the pieces around the dish and get a treat when he happens upon something edible.

Rope perches are fine, but you must watch for and eliminate any loose strands that could entangle your parrotlet.

Many parrot experts recommend using full-spectrum lightbulbs to ensure that your bird is getting enough vitamin D.

Perches

The cage you purchased will likely have come with a few plastic perches or a couple of wooden dowels, and though those are fine perches to use, it's an inadequate selection. Because your parrotlet uses his feet all day, it's important that he have as many different perch widths, materials, and textures to stand on as possible. If your bird has only one type and size of perch to stand on, he can develop serious foot problems. Think of good perches like orthopedic shoes. Choose hard wooden perches with natural bends and twists and variations in diameter.

You can use perches harvested from trees available to you, but you must be absolutely certain that the type of tree is nontoxic and that it was never sprayed with insecticide. Though your parrotlet will enjoy chewing on this "green" wood, he shouldn't be exposed to toxins. Apple trees and citrus trees are safe, as long as they haven't been sprayed with any chemicals. Boxwood, holly, locust, and red maple are some common trees that are toxic and therefore unsafe to use as perches. Other trees may or may not be safe; consult your veterinarian for information on the safety of specific trees.

If you use rope perches, be careful to trim all loose strands and make

Play Gyms

Parrotlets benefit from having a place to play away from the cage. Along with providing much needed out-of-cage playtime, a play gym is also a great taming tool because you can work with your bird on a perch away from his cage or in another room. Good gyms and play stands offer the same qualities as a well-designed cage in that they are sturdy and easily cleaned. Don't expect your parrotlet to stay on the play gym as a larger parrot would—he's more likely to come chasing after you, or will find some other mischief to get into while you're not looking.

Toy Safety

Not all toys are safe for your parrotlet. Remember, he has a very tiny head that can get caught in a small ring, and he could catch his delicate toes in odd places like the slots in a bell. Old toys with sharp edges or corners, frayed ropes, or loose strings can be hazardous as well. Be sure to quickly remove and replace any items that become worn or broken.

sure that the rope doesn't unravel. Loose stands can wind around a toe or foot and cause injury, and unraveled rope can create an area for the bird to insert his head and potentially get stuck.

Sand perches are available in a variety of colors and diameters and can often become a bird's favorite perch, especially for sleeping. This is a sand-covered rough perch that acts as a nail and beak trimmer. Every parrotlet should have at least one of these perches, but not to the exclusion of other types. Perches made of concrete also help keep nails trim.

You may find sandpaper sheaths that slip over existing perches—these were popular many years ago. These can become soiled and damp and may allow bacteria to grow that can be harmful to your bird's feet. Toss the sandpaper and use sand perches instead--they are easier to clean and much safer to use.

Electric warming perches are becoming popular now, especially for companion birds that live in colder climates. These plastic perches plug into a wall socket and emit a low-grade heat. Having one of them may

be good for your parrotlet if you live in a cold area –your bird is small and can easily become chilled.

Place perches well away from food or water dishes, not over them. This will help keep the dishes free of droppings (which will wind up in the water no matter what you do!). Don't place so many perches in the cage that your parrotlet can't move around. Leave him some space for exercise.

Play Gyms

A play gym, play stand, or jungle gym, consists of a platform provided with perches, ladders, and toys. This will give your bird an opportunity to play and get some much needed

Tucked In

Although some birds become frightened in the dark, others like to be covered at night. An appropriate cover can help eliminate nighttime drafts and will allow your parrotlet to sleep longer in the morning. In the wild, these tropical birds get about 12 hours of shuteye a day and should get about the same amount in the home.

activity, but don't expect to place your parrotlet on the stand and walk away—he probably won't be on it when you return! A play gym is also a great taming tool because you can place the bird on the steady perch and work with him there instead of trying to work with him close to his cage, where he might seek refuge.

Play gyms can get elaborate and expensive, but you can make one yourself out of a clay pot, some plaster of Paris, and some wooden dowels. Plug up the clay pot and fill it with plaster of Paris. Insert wooden dowels of various heights vertically into the plaster. Let the plaster dry, and then tie thinner dowels horizontally to the vertical dowels using sisal twine. Then tie wooden rings, unbleached paper cups, and plastic buttons all over the horizontal dowels at different levels.

Lighting

Parrotlets synthesize vitamin D in their bodies by spreading oil from a gland on their rumps (the uropygial gland) onto their feathers during preening. When the sun's rays hit this oil, it turns into a useable form of vitamin D, which the bird ingests during preening. If sunlight or light from a wide-spectrum bulb doesn't hit the feathers, he will not make this important vitamin and may become deficient. Invest in bird lamps if you live in a part of the country that gets cold and dark for a good portion of the year. You can get special full-spectrum light bulbs that mimic the sun's rays.

Some of these lamps are very expensive, and most are worth it, but you can find more inexpensive options. Buy a standard cheap spot lamp from the hardware store and

Cleaning Schedule

Your parrotlet's cage needs regular cleaning and maintenance in order to keep your bird healthy. Here's a sample cleaning schedule:

- Daily: Change paper in the tray; wash dishes with warm soapy water and rinse well.

- Weekly: Remove perches and scrub them in warm soapy water, then rinse and dry well. Remove the bottom grate and tray and wash well, removing all debris. Remove all toys and check them for broken parts or unraveled rope, then wash and dry them.

- Monthly: Dismantle the cage if you can and wash it with soapy water, or place the whole thing in the bathtub or take it outside. Soak in a 10 per cent bleach solution if it's very crusty.

Youngsters and Bird Care

No matter how much a child promises that he or she will take care of a pet *no matter what*, it's critical that an adult in the household be the pet's primary caretaker, allowing the child the privilege of supervised care. Watch to make sure that the child is feeding his pet bird every day and cleaning the paper. You will have to take over more in-depth cage cleaning chores. Remember, a 10-year-old might be 30 or older by the time the parrotlet departs for greener pastures (or bluer skies). A parrotlet might get lost in the shuffle of growing up and going to college and other life changes.

place it a few feet away from your parrotlet's cage. If you can't find bird-specific bulbs, use bulbs made for reptiles–they are very similar. Ideally, the light from the lamp should come from above, so use a hanging fluorescent lamp fixture if it's convenient.

Bedding

The best thing to put into the birdcage tray is plain old newspaper. There's some evidence that shows that the ink in the paper actually has antibacterial properties. Your cage should have a grate to prevent your bird from getting to the soiled paper. If it doesn't, consider getting another cage.

Other types of bedding are not recommend for birds, including corncob bedding, walnut shells, newspaper pellets, rabbit food pellets, and wood shavings. These items aren't necessarily bad for the birds, but they do hold moisture and can allow bacteria and fungus to grow much faster than newspaper. Also, since some of these types of bedding

look like bird food (small pellets) your parrotlet may ingest it and become ill from crop impaction or another ailment.

It's also easier to see when newspaper is dirty, and much harder to see the filth with other kinds of bedding. Also, if you ever need to take your bird to the veterinarian because you think he's ill, you can easily show the vet the droppings on the paper–not so with the other bedding. And used newspaper is free! If you don't want to use newspaper, simple paper towels will do as well, as will plain newsprint paper you can buy at craft stores.

Seed Catcher

Some cages come with skirts that catch a good deal of fallen food and waste. If your cage doesn't have them, you can buy a cage "bloomer," acrylic panels, or other plastic guards. These items do work to keep much of the mess inside the cage, but they're not perfect. You will still need to do some floor cleaning. Plastic or acrylic cages help keep in a lot of the mess; just make sure they are well ventilated.

Grooming Supplies

Bathing is good for your parrotlet's skin and is a natural behavior that should be encouraged. Most birds will bathe in their water dish. You can provide your parrotlet with a separate bath that he may prefer. A shallow saucer filled with warm water often does the trick. You don't need to use commercially prepared spray baths—they may contain elements that can irritate your bird's eyes. It's probably best to stick with plain bottled water.

If you're going to be trimming your parrotlet's nails and wings yourself, you will need the correct type of clippers and scissors. (Please see Chapter 4 for more details on these essential items.)

Bird Spa

Putting a special suction-cupped perch on your shower wall is a great way to spend more time with your parrotlet and gives him a steamy spa treatment that's great for his feathers and skin. Be careful, however, to prevent him from getting burned by keeping the water temperature on the cooler side in case he inadvertently flies into the stream. Also, close the toilet lid, and never leave him unattended. Put him back into his cage if you're going to use a blow dryer or flatiron, as both may contain nonstick elements that can cause noxious fumes.

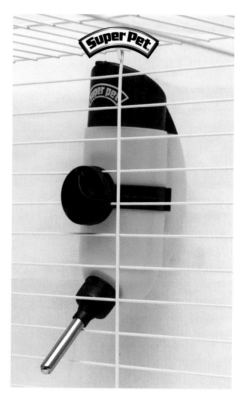

Some parrotlets will use a water bottle, although you should still supply a water bowl.

Cage Cleaning and Supplies

Many household cleansers are deadly to your bird, so don't use any chemicals in or around his cage. Instead, use natural disinfectants such as vinegar for cleaning and baking soda for scrubbing. You can use a 10 percent bleach solution for soaking components of the cage, but make sure to rinse very carefully. Grapefruit seed extract also makes a great disinfectant, and you only need 32 drops per quart and a cheap spray bottle. This extract is safe to ingest and can be used all over the house.

Cuttlebone and Mineral Block

The cuttlebone is a standard item in most parrotlets' housing. It is actually the internal shell of certain squids. The cuttlebone provides calcium and other essential minerals, as well as providing the parrotlet with another fun chewing activity.

A mineral block and a beak block are essentially the same thing: a lump of minerals shaped into a block or another fun shape. Your parrotlet will appreciate this treat, and it will help to keep his beak trim while adding some calcium and minerals to his diet.

Cage Cover

If your bird's chirping bothers you early in the morning, consider getting a cage cover. Many companies make them for standard cage sizes, or you can have one custom-made. You can also toss a dark sheet or piece of fabric over the cage as well. Keep an eye out for any fraying or holes in the cover. Your bird can pull at part of the cover or at hanging threads from inside the cage and potentially strangle himself with them.

Travel Carrier

Even if you don't plan on taking trips with your parrotlet, you will need a travel carrier in case of emergencies. Small bird carriers typically have a door on the top for easy access. They should be easy to clean and small enough to fit beneath the seat of an airplane. They should also have adequate ventilation and a place to put food and water dishes.

A travel carrier is essential for taking your parrotlet to the vet's office.

3

Feeding Your Parrotlet

Just like humans, parrotlets need a good-quality diet packed with nutrition in order to stay healthy. Avian nutrition has come a long way in the past two decades, and today we know much more about what makes parrots "tick" than before. As it turns out, a "convenient" diet isn't the best diet for companion birds. It's easy to open a bag of seeds and dump them into a coop cup, but that type of simple diet is deadly for a parrotlet. Sure, it can survive in the short term on birdseed alone, but just like a person being fed only bread and water, it's just a matter of time before malnutrition and disease become an issue. Yes, seed may still be a part of a parrotlet's diet–these little birds relish seed–but it's only part of a larger nutritional plan.

The Best Nutrition

Your parrotlet needs many of the same nutrients that you need to be healthy. Here are just four of the many important vitamins, minerals, and dietary nutrients that your parrotlet requires.

Protein

Protein is required for feather, beak, and toenail production and health, as well as being an important part of building and maintaining muscle and other organs. There is some protein in seeds and pellets, but you can also offer well-cooked scrambled eggs, plain yogurt, and even some bits of well-done chicken.

Calcium

Calcium is necessary for bones and body function; lack of calcium can cause seizures; deficiency can also cause egg binding in female parrotlets, especially those that consistently lay eggs the year around. For birds, calcium is available in fortified products, some fresh greens, carrots, and almonds. It can also be supplemented in the diet by offering cuttlebone and mineral blocks.

Vitamin A

Vitamin A is an essential vitamin for birds because it promotes respiratory and liver health. It found in leafy greens and orange vegetables, which your parrotlet may enjoy. It

Broccoli is a good source of calcium for your parrotlet.

Feeding Tips

Parrotlets can feed all day, and their metabolism requires food to be available at all times. Unlike as with dogs and cats, you should not remove food from your bird's housing once you feed him. Offer the healthiest foods in the morning when he's hungry, however, to make sure he's ingesting the most nutritious offerings. For example, make a fruit and veggie salad in one bowl, and offer a cooked diet and some table foods in another. In the evening, offer seeds and pellets. That way the bird will have already filled up all day on the good food and can have the fun stuff in the evening. Since you won't remove the dish of seed or pellets, your bird can pick through their remains during the day if he doesn't like the other food you've served. Remember that parrotlets hull their seeds, so what may look like a full dish of seeds might actually be a full dish of husks.

is also found in red palm oil, which you can use in small amounts on your parrotlet's moist foods. Do not supplement vitamin A without a veterinarian's supervision, as too much can be toxic, especially for birds this small.

Vitamin C

Vitamin C is necessary for the immune system. For parrotlets, vitamin C is available in kale, red peppers, strawberries, and oranges.

Variety Is the Key

Imagine if you ate just one or two foods day after day. Eventually you'd suffer from a dietary imbalance that may create disease or a breakdown of some of the systems in your body. The same holds true for companion birds. The key to their health is to vary the types of healthy foods that they eat, including fresh vegetables and fruits, grains, and supplements.

Birds are relatively similar to humans in their dietary requirements. On the whole, they do need a bit more attention paid to their calcium and vitamin A intake (they seem to need more than we do respective to their size), but beyond that all you have to do is offer a wide variety of foods; the trick is getting your parrotlet to eat them. The good news is that parrotlets aren't known to be as picky as some other species, so if you keep offering the right kinds of foods, your bird will probably let curiosity get the better of him and try them.

What Wild Parrotlets Eat

The wild parrotlet in Mexico and Central and South America consumes primarily young seeds and fruits. It is unlikely that your parrotlet will get a diet quite like this in your home, but you can get as close to it as possible by offering a wide variety of fresh foods that will give the bird similar nutrients to what he would be eating in the wild.

Parrotlets require a varied diet that contains many different types of seeds, vegetables, fruits, and other items.

Bird Seed

Companion parrotlets won't thrive on a all-seed diet, but seeds combined with other nutritious foods can create a balanced diet. An all-seed diet will cause your parrotlet to develop serious health issues and will shorten his lifespan by well more than half. A parrotlet may live to over 20 years of age, but will only live to be about 5 or 6 on an all-seed diet. Birds do get fat, even though it's hard to tell what's going on beneath their feathers. An obese parrotlet will eventually have health problems and diseases, including fatty tumors, respiratory problems, and musculoskeletal issues. Tumors can ulcerate and require surgery, if your bird doesn't die first.

Seeds are not a bad or unhealthy food, but they are generally misused. Many veterinarians suggest that people eliminate seeds from their birds' diet because they feel that owners may not be responsible enough to provide a varied and nutritious diet for their pets. Seeds do provide a lot of carbohydrate and fat to your bird's diet, things that a wild parrotlet needs far more than the companion parrotlet does. Offering seeds is certainly easy, but putting a little extra effort into what you feed your parrotlet will save you some high veterinary bills in the future.

You can give your parrotlet seed in small amounts, but not as a total diet. A seed blend can make up 20 to 30 percent of your parrotlet's diet. Your veterinarian may suggest that you don't feed seed at all, but that choice is yours. Your parrotlet will certainly enjoy it, and seed does provide some essential nutritional components to his diet.

Choosing the right kind of seed is easy. Look for a seed with a cockatiel's face on the bag, or one that says it's for cockatiels and/or lovebirds. Even though your parrotlet is small, do not choose a parakeet mix. Parakeets won't eat some of the ingredients in the lovebird blend, but your parrotlet will enjoy them. Most seed mixes that are appropriate for parrotlets contain millet, sunflower seeds, oat groats, safflower seeds, buckwheat, nyjer seed, corn, canary grass seeds, rape

The Importance of Exercise Combined with Diet

How does the wild parrotlet thrive? It has an important advantage over your companion parrotlet: plenty of exercise. Wild parrotlets fly a lot during the day looking for food. These wild birds are genetically programmed for this kind of strenuous exercise, and it makes them hardy and strong. It's likely that your parrotlet isn't getting this kind of workout. Even if he lives in a large aviary, it's impossible to mirror the environment of the wild parrotlet. Nevertheless, well-cared-for companion parrotlets can live longer than their wild counterparts because no predators are lurking around in the average home—well, except the family cat!

seed, flax seed, and others mixed into a blend. If you've got a feed store nearby, you can create your own mix with the seeds that your parrotlet likes the best so that there's less waste. All-in-one mixes do not suit every bird.

Brightly colored vitamin-fortified seed mixes look and smell pretty, but the vitamins are in the coloring that the manufacturer coats on the outside of the seed. The inside, the only part that your parrotlet actually eats, remains uncoated, and therefore unfortified. Save your money and buy the plain-looking seed at a feed store and spend the difference on healthy fruits and vegetables for your bird. The regular seed is not as colorful, but it's less expensive and is just as good.

Sprouting Seeds

Since wild parrotlets eat young seeds in the wild, as opposed to the mature seeds you find in the pet store, you may want to try sprouting some of the mature seeds to see whether your parrotlet will eat them. Seeds that have been sprouted are much higher in nutrition than dry seeds, so if you have time you can make your bird's favorite seeds into a healthy treat that you can serve every day.

A seed mix formulated for cockatiels or lovebirds is appropriate for parrotlets.

Is Grit Important for Digestion?

Grit is a popularly sold dietary supplement available in any pet store; it usually comes in a rectangular box. There are two types: soluble, like oyster shells and cuttlebone, and insoluble, like silica. A common and persistent myth says that parrots need grit in their diet. Most parrots, including your parrotlet, that eat a healthful varied diet will not need any form of grit. Parrotlets hull their seeds, meaning they eat the meat from inside the shell, so they don't need little pebbles inside of their gizzard to help grind their food. However, there is evidence to show that small amounts of grit can aid digestion. Freely feeding grit is not recommended, however, because too much grit can cause crop impaction, which can be fatal. Offering small amounts of soluble grit once a week is acceptable, but is not necessary. I'd recommend staying away from it.

Remember in elementary school when you sprouted dry beans in a jar? Sprouting seed is that easy. You can buy sprouted beans at the supermarket, or you can sprout seeds and beans on your own using a sprouting kit from any health food store. Some companies sell a sprouting kit for birds that you can use right out of the box.

You don't need a green thumb to follow these simple steps:
• Rinse the seeds and soak them overnight in cool clean water.
• Line the bottom of a shallow flat dish with wet paper towels and spread the seeds in a single layer on top of them.
• Cover the dish with plastic wrap and punch several holes in it.
• Place the pan somewhere warm where it will also receive light.
• Make sure that the paper towels don't dry out.
• In 3 to 5 days, when the seeds are sufficiently sprouted, rinse them in cold water and store them in the refrigerator.

Sprouted seeds spoil quickly, so keep an eye on them. Actually, keep a "nose" on them—sprouts that are going bad will have a foul odor. Don't offer your parrotlet rancid or moldy seed. If you notice an odor coming from the seeds or they feel sticky, toss them out. A good trick is to put a few drops of grapefruit seed extract into the water of your last rinse. You can find it in any health food store or online. This extract is perfectly safe for use with birds and has some healthful benefits, such as antibacterial, antifungal, and antiviral properties. You can even put a couple of drops of it into your bird's water a few days a week (but not every day).

Pelleted Foods

Pellets emerged on the avian dietary scene in the 1990s and have become a prominent trend in feeding parrots. Pellets are a combination of healthful ingredients, including seeds and grains, that the manufacturer shapes into bits that resemble seeds and other foods that birds find interesting, similar to the way some dog and cat foods are made using an extrusion process. Though pellets do contain some good stuff, there has been a backlash recently against the feeding of pellets as a total diet, the same way there was a backlash against using seeds as a total diet. Long-term use of a pellet-only diet has shown results similar to long-term use of an all-seed diet, so it's important to give your bird some variety.

As with seeds, pellets are not bad, but they are not the only food you should feed your parrotlet. Pellets are a good base diet, but feeding them does not mean that you should exclude other foods, such as fruits and vegetables, table foods, and some seeds. Along with other healthy foods, pellets are nutritious and can compose 50 percent of your bird's total diet.

To choose the right pellets for your parrotlet, check the label and try to buy only all-natural, preservative-free, organic pellets in a small size that's appropriate for your bird. Pellets that are brightly colored or smell very fruity may have additives that aren't healthful for your bird, so read the label first (though birds often find these types of pellets palatable and are fine if your parrotlet likes them).

Sprouted seeds are more nutritious than regular seeds, and sprouting seeds for your parrotlet is not difficult.

You might notice that the seed mix you use has these types of pellets in it. Again, be aware of what your parrotlet is actually eating out of the seed mix. You may be paying for pellets that your bird isn't consuming, which is a waste of money. The best pellets for your parrotlet are the ones that he will actually consume—a bowl of unconsumed pellets is a waste of your money and can frustrate your bird.

The debate about pellets and seeds has divided bird owners. Some won't touch seeds and others won't touch pellets. It's best to fall somewhere in between to be able to offer your bird the best possible diet and nutritional choices, as well as giving him fun stuff to eat.

Seeds given in moderation are not going to harm your bird. Pellets can be a great base diet if you also offer other foods. Use your own judgment and the advice of your veterinarian. If you have decided to convert your parrotlet from a seed-based diet to a pellet-based diet, get the go-ahead from your avian veterinarian first. Conversion can be stressful, and your parrotlet should be in prime condition before you make the switch.

After your veterinarian approves the switch, mix the pellets with the seed in a 50/50 ratio so that your parrotlet gets used to seeing the pellets. Gradually reduce the ratio of seeds to pellets each week, until you're feeding only pellets by the fifth or sixth week. Keep offering lots of other foods at this time as well, especially fruits, vegetables, and cooked foods. Make sure that your parrotlet is actually eating the pellets before you completely remove seed from his diet. Parrotlets can starve to death and can otherwise be severely affected by not eating for as little as a day and a half.

Never try to convert breeding birds or sick birds, and never make your parrotlet switch cold turkey. Younger parrotlets will have

Like other small parrots, parrotlets tend to be very fond of millet spray.

Offer your parrotlet several varieties of fruits and vegetables daily.

an easier time converting than older parrotlets, so start early. Some pet stores or breeders wean their birds onto pellets, so be sure to ask about the bird's diet before you bring him home. It's likely that your parrotlet has been weaned onto seed.

Pesticides

It's important to remember to thoroughly rinse all produce before offering it to your bird. His body is small, and the slightest traces of pesticides could endanger him. Feed organic fruits and veggies if you can.

Fruits and Vegetables

Vegetables and fruits are critical to including important vitamins and minerals into your parrotlet's diet. Considering that your parrotlet would be eating fruit in the wild, not adding fruit and veggies to your bird's diet is a big mistake. Most companion parrotlets don't have a lot to do all day, so playing with different kinds of fruits and vegetables also offers a great distraction. Try to feed at least four to six fresh vegetables and fruits a day, and more if you can. Eventually you'll get to know what your parrotlet's favorites are and you can keep them on hand to offer every day.

Fresh Veggies and Fruits

The types of fresh vegetables and fruits you can offer your parrotlet include, but are not limited to, the ones listed below.

Vegetables:

asparagus

beans (cooked)

bell peppers (any color)

broccoli

cabbage

carrot

cauliflower

celery

cilantro

corn

cucumber

endive

green bean

greens (all kinds)

hot peppers

kale

okra

parsley

peas

potato (cooked)

pumpkin

radicchio

rapini

snow peas

spinach

sprouts

squahses

sweet potato (cooked)

tomato

turnip

watercress

yams

zucchini

Fruits:

apple

apricot

banana

berries (any kind)

fig

grapes

guava

kiwi

mango

melons (any kind)

nectarine

orange

papaya

peach

pear

pineapple

plum

pomegranate

prickly pear

tangerine

Preparation

The best fruits and vegetables for your parrotlet are deep green or orange in color. This type of produce has the most nutrients, especially vitamin A, which your parrotlet needs to maintain a healthy respiratory system. Vitamin A-deficient birds are prone to respiratory, skin, and liver problems.

Wash all fruit and vegetables thoroughly before serving them to your parrotlet. His body is tiny and can be affected by even the smallest traces of pesticides. Offer organic produce if you can so that you have one less thing to worry about.

Fruits and vegetables sour quickly in warm weather, so remove them before they spoil and replace them with a new batch if it's convenient. You can leave fruits and veggies with the bird longer in cooler weather, but make sure to remove them in the evening without fail.

What To Do if Your Parrotlet Won't Eat Them

Offering the fruits and vegetables is the easy part. Getting your bird interested in eating them is tricky, even though parrotlets aren't known to be extremely picky. Try chopping, grating, or slicing the fruits and vegetables, or offering the food whole. Clipping greens to the side of the cage is a great way to get your

If your bird won't eat a certain food, try chopping it in a different shape or presenting it differently.

parrotlet interested in them. Be patient. Offer new things week after week. Parrotlets are curious and will eventually try the new food. Offer carrots chopped, sliced, and shredded. Try serving various types of greens in shallow dishes that have water in the bottom. Some birds will bathe in the greens and then dine on them. Each bird's preferences are different. If your parrotlet is being fussy about his food, try offering smaller or larger pieces or changing his feeding dishes.

If your parrotlet is still fussy after a few weeks of offering a variety of new foods, perhaps it's because he's afraid of the dish you're using, or he's not happy with the way you're offering the food. Perhaps the food is too big or too small. Change the bowls. Cook the vegetables. You can even bake or cook fresh veggies and fruit into breads, casseroles, scrambled eggs, and other meals. If you're pressed for time, use frozen vegetables and fruits–they aren't as good as using fresh produce, but if that's all you have time for on a particular day, they are better than nothing. Never used canned veggies, however, because they contain too much salt. Also, feed citrus only three days a week, because acidic fruits should be fed in moderation.

Cooked Diet

Another good addition to your base diet (seeds or pellets) is a cooked diet,

Your parrotlet needs constant access to fresh, clean drinking water.

which you can buy commercially or make on your own. These diets contain grains, dehydrated veggies and fruits, and supplements. They are easy to cook and keep in the refrigerator for a week. Most parrotlets will love picking through a bowl of warm cooked grains, beans, and rehydrated veggies.

If you want to make a cooked diet yourself, soak and cook a few types of beans (kidney, lentil, white, garbanzo, etc.), or used canned beans in a pinch, cook three or four types of healthy grains (brown rice, amaranth, barley, red wheat, quinoa, whole oats, etc.), cook up a batch of couscous, and lightly sauté some veggies, like kale, carrots, yams, tomato, and parsley in olive oil. Mix everything together, put some in the refrigerator for use during the next week, and freeze the rest in small baggies for your daily portions beyond the week. Thaw before serving. If you're using the microwave to thaw your mixture, make sure there are no hotspots in the food before you serve it. To get your parrotlet used to eating a cooked diet, sprinkle his favorite seeds over the mixture to attract him to the bowl.

If you enjoy baking, you can also make "birdy bread" simply by adding healthy veggies, pellets, nuts, and other items to commercially prepared corn muffin mix. Only feed this to healthy birds that have no history of yeast infection. This is more of a treat than a base diet, but you can offer it a couple of times a week and it freezes well.

Table Foods

Healthy table foods can be a healthy addition to your parrotlet's diet. With very few exceptions, your bird can eat anything and everything that you eat. Don't worry about spices–birds can eat the hottest of peppers because they have fewer taste receptors on their tongues.

A good rule for table foods for birds is that if it's good for you, it's probably good for the bird (with the exception of avocado, chocolate, alcohol, and caffeine, which are toxic to birds) and if it's bad for you, it's probably bad for the bird too. So, though junk food is tasty, the salt and fat can be deadly to your little parrotlet. Don't feed your parrotlet anything greasy either.

Eggs offer a lot of nutrients, and most birds usually love them (it does seem a little cannibalistic, but try not to think about it!). Boil eggs for about 30 minutes, cool them, and then crush them, shell and all. Make sure to boil the eggs well, because those eggs came from a chicken that could potentially pass a disease on to your parrotlet. If you're a whiz in the kitchen (or even if you're not), you can scramble eggs with some pellets or fresh chopped veggies. Add some grated soy cheese for some extra protein (a bird's digestion isn't equipped to handle cheese or any other dairy products).

Whole wheat and nutty grain bread are great additions to the diet. Unsalted whole wheat crackers are good, too. Unsalted peanut or almond butter spread on the crackers or bread is a healthful treat as well. Whole wheat pasta in various shapes makes a nice meal, especially if you add grated veggies and other grains.

Your parrotlet can even eat well-cooked flesh meats, like chicken and fish, but in moderation. Offer these

Toxic Foods

Although birds can basically eat what we eat, be aware that some foods are toxic to them and can be fatal: salty/sugary/fatty foods, pits and fruit seeds, chocolate, mushrooms, dried beans, avocado, raw onions, alcohol, caffeine, and carbonated beverages.

meats no more than two times a week. Too much protein isn't ideal for your parrotlet's diet, but you can feel free to occasionally share your chicken sandwich.

Fresh Water

Fresh, clean, chemical-free water is essential for your parrotlet. Parrotlets have very small bodies, and the build-up of metals and toxins happens much more quickly than in humans, so try not to use water straight from the tap. It probably contains chlorine, which can leach important nutrients from your bird's body. Bottled drinking water or filtered water is a much better option.

Change your bird's water no less than twice a day. Dirty water is full of bacteria that are potentially harmful for your bird. Water dishes should be clean enough for you to drink out of them. Soak them in a 10 percent bleach solution (90 percent water) once a week to sterilize them. Be sure to rinse them thoroughly before returning them to your parrotlet's cage. Change the water each and every day, even two or three times a day if he tends to toss things into it. Even if you have a tube-style waterer, you must change the water daily or risk your parrotlet's becoming ill.

Healthy Treats

Treats are a fun part of your parrotlet's dietary regimen and can add a lot of nutrition as well. A commercially produced pressed seed/pellet treat is always relished. Parrotlets love

millet spray too, but it doesn't offer a whole lot of nutrition, so offer only a couple a week. Air-popped popcorn is a healthful and fun snack. Sprinkle it with a little olive oil and some nutritional yeast to pack it full of nutrition. Cranberries and blueberries placed in a shallow bowl are fun because they roll around and present a little bit of a challenge.

Foraging Foods

"Foraging" is the latest trend in avian nutrition. Research and anecdotal evidence shows that birds who work for their food as they would in the wild are more mentally stimulated than birds who don't, which is important for their physical health as well. There are some fun foraging products on the market, many of which include a seed/pellet mixture pressed into wood and other toys.

A "birdy kabob" is also a great way to get your little feathered friend to eat his greens and "forage" for them as well. Simply thread small bits of vegetables and fruits onto the kabob, which you can get at most bird stores, and hang it in the cage. This gives your parrotlet the feeling of having to "work" for his food.

A Sample Diet

Here's an idea of how easy it is to create a wholesome diet for your parrotlet.

Choose one day a week in which you'll cook for your bird. Make a commercially prepared or homemade

Supervised Feeding

Parents of young children should always supervise a pet's care. Even though a parrotlet might be a child's companion, his nutritional needs are best left to adults. A child may forget to feed a pet, and a parrotlet can die after a couple days of starvation. A child can definitely help with the parrotlet's care, however, by measuring out the bird's dry food ration for the day, or if the child is old enough to help in the kitchen, he or she can wash fruits and veggies and offer them to the bird once an adult has prepared them.

mix of beans, grains, and veggies, and freeze it into seven portions. Freezing does eliminate some of the nutritional value, but you'll make up for that with the fresh foods that you offer. Each example should provide enough food for your parrotlet for a day, but every bird is different, so adjust accordingly.

Example #1

Thaw one portion of the cooked diet and put it on one side of the bowl. On the other side, grate some carrot and add sliced apple, berries, and melon. In another dish, place chopped greens, turnips, red cabbage, and other veggies. The first dish will need to be removed in a few hours, or when you get home from work. The second dish will need to be removed before you go to bed. In the early evening, add 1/8 cup of seeds to your parrotlet's seed dish, and a couple of tablespoons of pellets (if you're offering only pellets, just add those and use seed as a treat three days a week). Add two drops of apple cider vinegar to the bird's water.

Example #2

Add the thawed cooked diet, along with a whole carrot, half an apple, grated beets, and some pear. In the veggie dish, include other types of greens, green beans, and broccoli. In another dish, offer a smashed hardboiled egg and perhaps some well-cooked chicken. Sprinkle nutritional yeast over everything. Later, add your seeds and pellets. Add probiotics to the water. (See the Dietary Supplements section for more information on probiotics).

Example #3

Use the thawed cooked diet, adding plums, chopped papaya, and half an orange to the dish. For veggies, choose pumpkin, hot peppers, and parsley. Offer a dish of cranberries and air-popped popcorn as a treat. Later in the evening, offer a millet spray along with the seeds and pellets. In the water, add two drops of grapefruit seed extract and a good-quality vitamin powder.

If you offer your parrotlet a healthy, balanced diet, supplements should not be necessary.

Example #4

On a day when you're swamped for time and have even run out of the cooked diet, thaw some frozen veggies, cut an apple in half, smash a hardboiled egg, and toss it all in the dish. On this day, add the seed/pellets at the same time.

Summing Up

As you can see, you can vary the fruits and veggies a lot, but always offer the cooked diet and the base diet every day in the evening, after your bird has had time to consume the better stuff. Table foods can be offered every day, but go easy on the protein-packed foods, offering them just two or three times a week.

Dietary Supplements

You may have seen vitamin or mineral supplements that go into your bird's water in your local pet shop. These companion-grade supplements will probably not harm your bird, but they shouldn't really be necessary if you provide a healthful balanced diet. Before you consider offering them, try to get your parrotlet to eat fruits and vegetables that are rich in vitamins, especially Vitamin A. These include carrots, sweet potatoes, kale, spinach, butternut squash, mangoes, red peppers, and turnip greens. You can supplement moist food by sprinkling spirulina or greenfood powder over it. Greenfood is powdered concentrated

Offering veggies on a birdie kabob turns food into a toy and encourages your parrotlet to try new things.

Supplements intended to be used in water can turn it into a "bacteria soup" in just a few hours, especially in warm weather.

If you do decide to occasionally add vitamins to your parrotlet's water, be sure that you change it frequently. Most veterinarians are opposed to water supplements for birds, but many keepers do find a good-quality one useful a couple of days a week. Many also add one or two drops of apple cider vinegar to the water daily; the acidity in it wards off bacteria and is healthful for your bird. Finally, adding a couple of drops of grapefruit seed extract to the water a few days a week helps to ward off viruses, fungi, and bacteria.

Bee pollen is also a good addition to your parrotlet's diet. Since parrotlets in the wild eat flowers and buds, they are also ingesting some pollen as well. Bee pollen can be found in most health food stores.

One easy way to add supplements to your parrotlet's moist foods is to put all of the powdered ingredients into a cheese shaker (like one you'd see at a pizza restaurant), including spirulina, powdered probiotics, and bee pollen, and keep it in the fridge for freshness.

greens, and spirulina is a highly nutritious algae.

Probiotics, like acidophilus, are great to help balance the bird's digestive and immune system and can be offered in the water a few days a week, or sprinkled over moist foods.

Grooming
Your
Parrotlet

4

Parrotlet grooming isn't like dog grooming—you don't need to take your bird anywhere for fancy baths and spa treatments. Your parrotlet will groom himself as a matter of routine during his daily activities. He will "preen" himself by running his beak through his feathers to make sure they are orderly and clean. There will still, however, be a few grooming tasks you'll need to address, either by performing them yourself or by having your veterinarian perform them.

All About Feathers

Feathers are made up of the *rachis*, or shaft, onto which smaller strands, or *barbs*, are attached. The barbs are lined with even smaller strands, the *barbules*, which are lined with little *hooklets*. The hooklets and the barbules act like Velcro to stick the barbs together (though the fluffy white down feathers near the bird's skin don't have these features). Once stuck together, the feathers look smooth and cohesive. Feathers are delicate, but when they work together they are strong enough to challenge gravity and give the bird flight. When a bird preens, he is making sure that each part of each feather is neatly "stuck" together and that each feather is in its place.

Feathers also help to insulate the bird against the cold by keeping warm air close to the skin. If the feathers become dirty or the bird gets into something sticky or oily, his ability to regulate his temperature is compromised. That is why it's so important for birds to keep their feathers in prime condition. Feathers are made mostly of a protein called keratin, the same substance as our fingernails. For a bird to have the optimum feather quality, he must have an optimum diet.

The parrotlet has a gland at the base of the tail at the top of the rump called the uropygial gland, which secretes oil that he gathers with his

Like other parrots, parrotlets spend a lot of time preening to keep their feathers in top condition.

beak during preening and spreads throughout his feathers. This oil keeps the feathers supple and water-resistant. It also contains elements that are the precursors to vitamin D--when sunlight hits the oil on the feathers, it creates vitamin D, which the bird then consumes as it preens. Isn't nature amazing? This gland can become infected and diseased, largely due to the lack of a good diet—another reason why it's important to feed your parrotlet correctly.

Bathing

Parrotlets need to bathe to keep their feathers clean and their skin moist. Most will happily bathe themselves and won't need help from you, aside

Feather Loss

Molting is a bird's way of replacing feathers that are worn out. The bird will systematically lose feathers from all over his body, but not all at once, and not in patches—bald patches are a sign of illness or a behavioral issue that needs to be addressed immediately. You will notice during a molt more feathers on the bottom of the cage than usual and will see pin feathers (see "Clipping the Feathers" section for more on pin feathers) emerging from between the other feathers. Molts occur once or twice a year and can last a few months. Offer your bird a nutritious diet at this time to help with feather production, and include some extra protein.

from being given a shallow dish filled with clean water in which to bathe. If the drinking dish is large enough, your parrotlet will try to bathe in it, which is fine, but you should also offer a separate bathing dish a couple of times a week, perhaps even more often. The dish should be shallow and not easy to tip over. Add about an inch (2.5 cm) of tepid water. Birds prefer to bathe in cooler water (but not freezing cold).

You might not think that bathing in winter is a good idea, but your home may be too dry from heating, and the bird will need to keep his skin moisturized. Dry skin can lead to itching and feather chewing and plucking, so be sure to provide plenty of opportunity for bathing. Remove the bowl in the evening and dry the cage and surrounding area thoroughly after a bath.

Fresh clean bottled water makes the best bath. You can buy spray bath items from the pet store, but they are not necessary, and some can even irritate the bird's eyes or nasal passages. Some people occasionally add a few drops of glycerin to the water to make the bird shiny, but that's not necessary either.

Misting

Some parrotlets like being misted or sprayed from above. It's easy enough to provide this experience by using an inexpensive spray bottle. Try to mist so that the water falls down like rain rather than spraying directly at the bird. Some parrotlets don't like this

Most parrotlets are happy to bathe themselves. You only need to provide yours with a shallow dish of water.

method, so don't force it on a resistant bird. You'll know whether your bird likes it when he rubs his head behind him, opens his wings, preens, and makes other bath-time motions. If you mist while he's still in the cage, remove his food dish and the paper beneath the tray and then replace them when you're done.

Showering

Bathing in your bathroom shower is great for a very tame bird. Get a suction-cup shower perch and place it above the water stream so that he can get to it or move away from it anytime he wants. Then take your shower as usual (but don't make the water too warm). You can also put the perch high above the shower and take a steamy shower. The moisture from the steam is great for the bird's skin. However, make sure the bird doesn't jump into the water; if he does, be ready to grab him immediately. Also, when he's in the bathroom, close the toilet lid and make sure that all toxic substances are put away. Remove from shelves anything that he could knock over in case he panics or flies. Remember that your parrotlet is very small and can drown easily. If you do shower with your bird, make sure that you keep an eye on him at all times.

The Kitchen Sink

Another fun place for the tame parrotlet to bathe is the kitchen sink. Remove everything from your clean sink and place a shallow dish at the bottom. Run a small stream of water from the tap into the dish and keep it running. Many birds will run down your arm and right into the sink! You may have to perch your bird on the edge of the dish, but don't force him if he's afraid. Show him the stream of water and encourage him to jump down into the sink. If he's not in the mood, try another day.

Drying Off

Your bird will dry on his own, but you can provide him with a spotlight lamp (ideally with a bird- or reptile-specific bulb) that will warm him as he preens. There's no need to blow-dry your parrotlet, especially since some blow dryers have non-stick coating on the heating coils, which can be dangerous and deadly. Blow-drying can also overheat a small bird.

Nail Care

Just like yours, a parrotlet's nails grow constantly. In fact, they are made of keratin, just like human nails. If they aren't worn down enough by perching, the nails will get sharp, making interaction with you unpleasant. Also, if they get too long, the toes will not curl correctly when gripping, which can cause foot problems.

Using concrete or sand perches of many sizes will help keep your bird's nails trim. Some birds will never need their nails cut. If yours does, you may want to consider a trip to

A shower perch allows you to bathe your parrotlet in the shower (shown here with a Quaker parrot).

Grooming Health Check

When grooming your bird, you should look for any abnormalities. Examine the face and feet. Check the bird's underside and beneath the wings for lumps, bumps, or sores. Feel the keel bone (it runs vertically along the bird's breast), and make sure that the bird isn't too thin: the keel should be prominent, but there should be flesh on either side of it. If it is very sharp, the bird is too thin; if you can't feel it at all, he may be too heavy or have a tumor there. If you get your bird groomed by an avian vet, he or she will give him a body check and will be able to detect whether something is amiss.

the veterinarian or a local bird shop that does grooming. It's very simple to trim the nails yourself, but you have to know how to hold the bird correctly in order not to hurt him.

The nail has two parts, just like human nails, the dead part of the nail (on the end), and the quick, where the blood supply is. Cut the dead part of the nail, never the quick. This is easy when you have a parrotlet with light-colored nails because you'll be able to see the vein in the nail and avoid it. If you have a bird with dark-colored nails, simply trim a very tiny amount off the tip of the nail rather than risk hurting your bird.

A human nail trimmer for babies works well for your parrotlet's little nails. A very small cat nail trimmer (guillotine style) is ideal. Keep styptic powder or cornstarch on hand at all times when trimming in case of bleeding. Simply dip the bird's nail into the powder, pull it out, and then tap the powder down into the nail.

Instead of clipping, you can make a few passes at your parrotlet's nails with a file once a week, which will keep them trim and eliminate the chances of hurting your bird. With clipping and filing, less is more—don't overdo it.

Trimming Tip

If you're not sure of how to hold your bird when trimming his nails, or you're nervous about it, you can use the "sneak up" method. Have the bird perch on one hand while you talk sweetly to him as a distraction, then sneak up on one toenail with a clipper and carefully snip off the very end—not too much! Then you're done for the day. Do this for eight days in a row and you'll clip all of the nails without any drama.

Beak Care

The parrotlet's beak is made of keratin, the same material as the nails, and is built over a honeycomb-like structure that makes it very light. A healthy bird does activities with his beak that will naturally wear it down, such as eating hard foods, playing with toys, wiping it on perches, and chewing on wood. If your parrotlet's beak seems overgrown, he may have a health disorder that needs to be addressed by a veterinarian.

Malnutrition can also cause the beak to overgrow. It is not advisable to trim your bird's beak, because you can severely injure your bird if you don't know what you're doing. If you notice something wrong with your parrotlet, please visit a veterinarian. Never, ever try to trim or file the beak on your own.

Wing Clipping

To prevent a bird from flying, some people trim the lower half of the primary flight feathers (the first ten feathers starting at the outside of the wing) off both of the wings. This practice is common among companion bird owners and is a painless procedure, much like getting a haircut. Like hair, the flight feathers do grow back, usually in about five to six months, or after a molt. If you want to keep your parrotlet's wings clipped, check the flight feathers every month or so to make sure none have grown out.

It is likely that you will not need to perform any beak maintenance other than offering your parrotlet hard foods and chewing toys.

Pros and Cons

Wing clipping is a much-heated discussion among bird enthusiasts. Here are the primary pros and cons:

Pro clipping: Safety–your parrotlet will not be able to fly away and get lost if you or someone in your household carelessly opens a window or a door, which happens frequently.

Con clipping: Safety–a clipped bird has no defense against predators in the home, like the family dog or cat.

Pro clipping: Temperament–a parrotlet that has its wings clipped is more manageable and sweet, more easily tamed and willing to stay tame.

Con clipping: Temperament–clipping a parrotlet takes away its "birdness." An unclipped parrotlet has more self-direction and is able to make choices in its life. It will choose to be with you when it wants, which is better than forcing it to do so.

Pro clipping: A bird is meant to live in a cage.

Con clipping: A bird is meant to fly.

Pro clipping: A home is not a safe place for a bird to fly. There are many dangers, including mirrors and closed windows, standing water, and toxic substances that an unclipped bird can find more easily than a clipped bird.

Con clipping: True, a home is not very safe for a bird to have full flight in; therefore a conscientious owner would build a flight cage or an aviary in which to offer his bird full flight.

Whether or not you clip your bird's wings depends largely on his housing and how you're going to be interacting with him. Many parrotlet owners do build aviaries and habitats for their birds. This is a great way to allow your birds to fly and get their necessary exercise. Flying is a wonderful psychological and physical experience for birds and is what they are meant to do. Some believe that taking that

Not a Kid's Job!

Children should not be responsible for any aspect of grooming the parrotlet, but they can certainly help to regularly clean and re-fill the bath dish and put it back inside the cage. They can also be at the veterinarian's office to soothe and calm the bird after nail or wing clipping.

away from them is akin to breaking someone's legs so that they can't move very far.

Clip for Training

That being said, an untamed parrotlet that you intend to tame does need to be clipped during the training process. If not, he's just going to fly away and you won't get any taming done. Once he's tame, if you have a good relationship and he likes being with you, you shouldn't need to clip him, as he will choose your company over sitting on top of the curtain rod. On the other hand, many households, especially those with children, aren't equipped to handle a flighted parrotlet, because of open windows and doors and other hazards. Only you know what kind of household you have and whether or not your bird is safer clipped or unclipped.

Clipping the Feathers

Learn to clip your parrotlet's wing feathers by watching someone experienced in clipping, like an avian veterinarian, a breeder, or a bird shop owner. You won't have to clip your bird yourself if you can find someone in your

area who will charge you just a few dollars. It's worth the effort and the cost not to have to do it yourself.

The wing clip should allow your parrotlet to flutter gently to the floor, not land with a thud. A severe wing clip can cause the bird to panic and not be able to navigate to the floor well. But if you cut too little, the bird could still take off into the sky, never to be seen again.

Clipping a parrotlet is a job for two people; one to hold the parrotlet in a small hand towel and one to clip the wings. The person clipping extends the wing carefully, holding it at the middle joint (equivalent to the elbow) and exposing the individual feathers. You will see the primary flight feathers at the end of the wing,

It's important to never clip a blood feather. Those shown in the photo are on an Amazon parrot, but a parrotlet's blood feathers look similar.

with shorter feathers, the coverts, covering the upper part of the flight–don't cut those shorter feathers! Cut the flight feathers parallel to the coverts, about two millimeters away from them. Parrotlets are light and are good flyers, so cut seven to ten of the flights to make sure yours can't still fly. For clipping, use a pair of small sharp scissors or a scissor-style cat claw trimmer, the type with a concave area on both blades, and cut one feather at a time, not all at once.

Clipping your parrotlet's wings helps keep him out of danger in your home, but some feel that it is unnatural and contributes to obesity.

Never, ever cut into a feather inside a sheath. This is a "living" feather and will bleed. Blood feathers, also called pin feathers, are newly grown feathers that still have a blood supply. Recognize blood feathers by the sheath of milky white material encasing them. If your parrotlet is light in color, you may even be able

How Much to Clip

Some owners decide to trim the lower half of their birds' primary flight feathers to prevent them from flying. It's important to keep in mind that clipping should allow your parrotlet to flutter gently to the floor. If you cut too much, there is potential for injury from falling. If you cut too little your bird could fly off into the wild blue yonder. Therefore it's best to have someone experienced like an avian veterinarian or breeder do it for you or teach you how to do it properly.

Molting

Grooming can be stressful for a bird, especially if you have to restrain him. But there's another aspect to grooming that can be pleasant for him: helping to remove feather sheaths. A single parrotlet doesn't have another bird to help him at molting time to remove feather sheaths on his head and face. All he can do it scratch at them. If your bird is very tame, have him sit on your shoulder or chest while you gently rub the sheaths between the tips of your thumb and forefinger. Not only does this feel good to the bird, it's nice bonding time. If he quarrels or gets agitated, just be gentler with your touch.

to see a vein inside the feather. Trim feathers in a clean, well-lighted place, and keep cornstarch on hand in case you accidentally clip a blood feather (don't use styptic powder; it can burn the skin). Or you can pull the bleeding feather out firmly but gently from the root; leaving it inside the wing can cause infection. When in doubt, visit your avian vet. Your parrotlet is too small for you to take any chances.

Trim the feathers on both wings evenly. Don't trim only one wing. That method does not allow the parrotlet to control its descent, and it could easily injure itself trying to land. Some people will advise you to leave the first two primary flight feathers intact, but this is not a recommended practice. Your parrotlet could break these feathers easily because the other feathers on the wing no longer protect them. The wing is strong as a cohesive unit, but the feathers themselves are easily breakable.

5

The Healthy Parrotlet

Parrotlets and other birds are complex organisms, and their bodies function somewhat differently from ours, with a delicacy that's sometimes startling. Overall the parrotlet is a hardy bird, but it does need a lot of TLC to remain healthy. Keeping an eye on your parrotlet's physical condition is an important part of being a good guardian and will save you on veterinary bills in the long run.

Finding an Avian Veterinarian

An avian veterinarian specializes in the care and treatment of birds. Birds are obviously quite different from dogs and cats and need a special doctor trained in the particular treatment of bird accidents, ailments, and diseases. A veterinarian who does not specialize in birds may not catch a subtle symptom or may not perform the proper tests. Just because your parrotlet is a tiny being doesn't mean that he needs less care than any other animal companion.

Take your new parrotlet to an avian veterinarian within three days of buying him. There are several good reasons for the visit:

- If you bought your parrotlet with a health guarantee from a shop, you will have some recourse if tests reveal that your new bird is ill.
- You will begin a relationship with the avian veterinarian, who will get to know your bird and be able to

Parrotlets are masters at hiding illness, so it's important to take yours to the vet for an annual checkup.

Poison Control

If you notice evidence of vomiting; paralysis; bleeding from the eyes, nares, mouth, or vent; seizures or shock and you're not able to get to an avian veterinarian right away, your parrotlet may have become poisoned. You may or may not actually see him come in contact with the poison—it could be an airborne pesticide used by a neighbor or he could've nibbled on a toxic houseplant when you weren't looking. Call the National Animal Poison Control Center's 24-hour Poison Hotline at (800) 548-2423, (888) 4-ANIHELP, or (900) 680-0000. If you can, try to discover what your bird has ingested so that they can better help you.

evaluate it better because he or she will have a "healthy reference" for him.

• Some avian veterinarians will not take an emergency patient unless the bird is a regular patient.

• Avian veterinarians often board birds in their offices, though some will board patients only.

• You will receive important recommendations from the vet, including about diet and housing.

• If your bird's beak, nails, or wings ever need trimming you will have a place to go that you trust.

The best way to find an avian veterinarian is by calling the Association of Avian Veterinarians at (561) 393-9801 or looking them up on the Internet at www.aav.org/search/. You can also ask the members of your local bird club or society about the veterinarians they use.

The Vet Visit

After the initial visit, you should take your parrotlet to the veterinarian for a yearly "well bird" checkup. Some people do this every six months, which isn't a bad idea. A small bird like the parrotlet can succumb in a very short time to illness, so it's best to catch any infections in their early stages. The money that you spend on these health checks will be far less than you have to spend on an emergency visit if you notice that your bird is ill.

Any change in attitude, behavior, physical appearance, or routine could be a sign of illness.

Vet Visit Jitters

Going to the doctor isn't fun for anyone, and a child may become concerned about what the veterinarian is going to do with his or her parrotlet. Explain that the visit is necessary to keep the bird happy and healthy. At most veterinary visits, the doctor will come into the office to speak with you and your child, but then take the bird into the back to conduct the testing. Prepare the child for this and let him or her know that the bird will come back. Bring some millet spray as a treat that the child can give the bird when the visit is over.

The veterinarian will give your bird a physical examination and weigh him. The average parrotlet will weigh between 28 and 35 grams, more or less. The doctor may take cultures from the bird's vent or mouth and take blood for testing. All of these tests show whether or not the bird is in good health, and they are absolutely necessary. Ask your vet which tests are being run and what they will indicate so you can stay informed.

General Signs of Illness

It's critical to be able to recognize the signs of illness in your bird. The first clue that most people get when their bird is ill is a change in attitude, behavior, or routine. There may be changes in the bird's vocalizations, where he stands in the cage, how much he sleeps, the quality of his breathing, and the quality of his tameness.

Parrotlets, like most other birds, appreciate routine, and a sudden break in it signals that you should at least investigate your bird's condition. Perhaps something has frightened him or the temperature has dropped or risen

Your parrotlet's ears are located just behind the eyes and are normally covered with feathers.

too much. There are possibilities other than illness. If you can't find any reason for your bird's unusual behavior, start looking for the following:

• Fluffiness: If you notice that your parrotlet has his feathers fluffed, he is trying to keep heat close to his skin and is having trouble regulating his temperature. Fluffiness might occur in conjunction with sleepiness, sleeping on two feet instead of one, or sleeping on the bottom of the cage.

• Sleeping too much: A parrotlet that is sick may sleep more than usual. Sleeping on the bottom of the cage is especially telling.

• Sleeping on two feet: A healthy bird generally sleeps standing on one foot.

• Loss of appetite: You should know how much and what your parrotlet is consuming each day. If you notice that your bird is not eating enough or if he stops eating, there is a problem.

• Attitude change: Your parrotlet might be ill if he seems listless and is not behaving in his usual manner.

• Lameness: If your bird can't use his feet, you can be guaranteed that there is a problem. Lameness can occur as a result of egg binding, injury, seizure, or other conditions.

• Panting or labored breathing: Either of these symptoms can indicate a respiratory ailment, or perhaps overheating.

• Discharge: If you notice any runniness or discharge from the eyes, nostrils, or vent, take your bird to the veterinarian immediately. A "wet"

Health Alert

A healthy parrotlet is usually active and vocal, and he keeps his feathers in good condition. An ill parrotlet may not keep up with grooming and "let himself go." He may also look sleepy and listless and spend a lot of time on the bottom of the cage. If you notice anything unusual over an extended period, seek veterinary attention promptly because a bird's condition can decline rapidly.

vent warrants investigation.

• Food stuck to the feathers around the face: This indicates vomiting or poor grooming, both possible signs of illness.

• Droppings change drastically: Your parrotlet's droppings should consist of a solid green portion, white urates (on top of the green), and a clear liquid. If any of these are discolored (darker green, black, yellow, or red) and there has been no change in diet, or you notice undigested food in the droppings, there might be an illness present.

Signs and Symptoms: What They Mean

Here are some more specific points to look for in both a healthy and an ill bird.

Eyes
A bird has one eye on either side of its head, allowing him to see almost

360 degrees around his environment. This helps him to watch for predators and other dangers. Birds also have a second eyelid that acts as a kind of squeegee for the eye, keeping it moist and clean. A healthy eye is clear, moist, and free of discharge. A parrotlet with an eye problem may squint or scratch it excessively with his foot, or will rub it on the perch or sides of the cage. Look for swollen eyelids, cloudy eyes, excessive blinking, discharge, and tearing.

Ears

Your parrotlet's ears are situated a short distance parallel to and behind the eyes and are covered by small feathers. You may get a glimpse of an ear after your parrotlet bathes, when the feathers around the head are wet and stuck together. Birds can't hear in the same range that we do, but they can hear in greater detail. If you can see your parrotlet's ear opening even if the bird isn't wet, make an appointment with your avian veterinarian.

Beak

Your parrotlet experiences much of its world through its beak and feet. The beak is made of the same durable material as our fingernails; it grows over a honeycomb-like structure that is basically hollow, a convenient design for an animal that needs to fly. The beak acts as a crushing tool but is also delicate enough to peel the skin off a pea. It also functions to help your parrotlet around, kind of like another foot. The cere, the fleshy place just above the beak, can sometimes become thick and rough in hens, a condition called brown hypertrophy. This is likely caused by hormones and

Sick Bay

Having a hospital cage on hand is important in case of emergencies and illnesses. It's a comfortable, warm, safe place for your parrotlet to calm down and recuperate. Line a 10-gallon (37.9-l) aquarium with paper towels and place a heating pad on low to medium underneath one-half of the aquarium—your bird must be able to move away from the heat if it gets too warm. Place a mesh cover on it and drape a towel over three-quarters of the tank. Place a *very* shallow dish of water (a weak bird can drown in even an inch of water) on one end, as well as some millet spray and seeds or pellets. Do not include toys or perches, but you may include a rolled-up hand towel for snuggling. Place the cage in a quiet location and clean the papers once a day or when they become soiled.

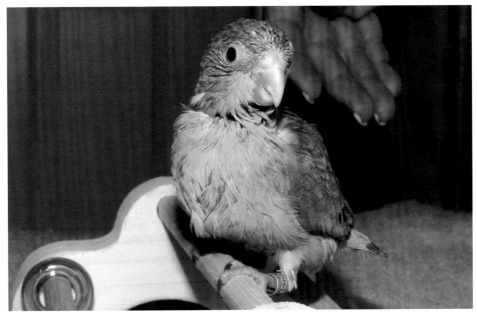

Parrots normally molt once or twice a year, but parrotlets are prone to molting year round, an unhealthy condition.

can be removed by a veterinarian. This is not a serious condition, but it should be treated nonetheless.

Feet

Parrotlet's feet are zygodactyl, meaning that they have two toes pointing forward and two toes pointing backward. This makes a parrotlet very adept at grasping and climbing. Birds also use their feet to regulate body temperature. During cold weather they can decrease the amount of blood circulating to their legs and will often draw one leg up into the body and stand only on the other. When parrotlets are warm, they will increase the blood flow to their legs to cool off.

Feathers

Feathers are one of the most amazing functional parts of a bird, helping him to fly, regulate temperature, and repel water. A healthy parrotlet should be obsessed with taking care of his feathers, preening them for much of the day.

Molting

Birds molt (also spelled moult) once or twice a year, usually during seasonal changes when sunlight becomes shorter or longer. Molting is the

Keep your parrotlet away from all smokes, fumes, and scents—his respiratory system is much more sensitive than yours.

themselves more often as the new feathers break out of their skin, and you may notice white "dandruff" on or around the cage; this is normal. When your bird is molting is not the time to try a new training method. A molting bird will appreciate a bath or spraying offered daily, with some aloe vera juice mixed in with the water.

Parrotlets are prone to a condition known as a "soft molt" or "unseasonal molt," where the bird molts all year around. This can happen to an ill bird or when the bird's environment isn't stable; changes in lighting and temperature can create a soft molt. To counteract this condition, make sure that your bird is getting only about 10 hours of light a day until the molting ends, and feed him lots of leafy greens and orange veggies at this time as well.

Feather Plucking

Occasionally parrotlets that have physical or psychological issues will pick at and chew their feathers, though in general parrotlets are not known as

process by which a bird loses some of the old feathers on his body and grows new ones. When your parrotlet molts, you will notice feathers on the bottom of the cage, but you should not be able to see patches of skin on his body. Molting birds might scratch

Toxic Cookware

Nonstick cookware emits toxic fumes when overheated, and these fumes are deadly to birds. Birds don't even have to be in the kitchen for the toxicity to overtake them—they can be anywhere in the home. There is no warning sign that birds are about to be overcome; they just drop off their perches dead. Just before this occurs, they may wheeze and gasp, but by then it's too late to save them. Small birds are especially susceptible. Avoid nonstick pots and pans, drip plates, burner drip pans, cookie sheets, light bulbs, and space heaters, just to name a few.

serious feather pickers or pluckers. If the cause is medical or nutritional, an avian veterinarian may help solve the problem. If it is psychological, you may have to be more diligent in caring for your bird and keeping him happy. A bird that is confined or kept in stressful situations may pick himself in order to relieve the stress or boredom. Provide your bird with enough space and toys and, of course, a trip to the veterinarian. Sometimes a cage-mate will pick out another bird's feathers. It's easy to tell whether this is going on because the feathers may be plucked on the top of the head, where the plucked bird can not reach. In this case, separate the quarreling birds.

Feather mites—seen here on a cockatiel—are not common in parrotlets but can be a problem for those kept outdoors.

Oiled Feathers

If your parrotlet becomes soaked in oil, it will no longer be able to regulate its body temperature, a condition that can be deadly. Dust the oil-soaked bird with cornstarch or flour and then gently bathe him in a small tub of warm water and some mild grease-fighting dish soap. Don't scrub the bird and don't wet his head! You may have to repeat this process several times. Keep the bird in a warm area until most of the oil is removed and the bird is dry.

Bleeding Feather

Sometimes a wing or tail feather will break in the middle of the growth process and begin to bleed. This is not a serious injury, though your parrotlet doesn't have much blood and can't afford to bleed even a few drops. Keep some cornstarch on hand in case of a bleeding emergency such as this one, and apply the product until the bleeding has stopped. Next you will need to remove the feather with a pair of needle-nosed pliers. While restraining the bird (you may need two people for this procedure), simply gently grasp the broken feather with the pliers, close to the shaft, and pull straight out. This will stop the bleeding and prevent infection. If you are too squeamish to do this yourself, take your parrotlet to your avian veterinarian. That may be preferable to your doing it yourself, because your parrotlet is very small and susceptible to injury.

Respiratory System

Your parrotlet has a delicate respiratory system that is sensitive to airborne irritants, such as aerosol sprays, fumes from heated nonstick cookware, and tobacco smoke. Birds don't breathe in the same way as humans. We inhale and exhale, completing one breath. Birds have to take two breaths for our one. The first breath fills the air sacs, situated in hollow spaces in the body and in some of the bones, and the second breath pushes the air into the lungs.

Birds are prone to respiratory illness and distress because their system is more complicated than ours. If you notice your parrotlet panting, call your avian veterinarian. Also, always be sure to keep him away from fumes and airborne toxins. You can recognize a respiratory infection by a change in breathing and, in extreme cases, bubbling from the mouth or nostrils. If you notice those symptoms, take your parrotlet to the veterinarian right away. An overheated bird will pant and spread its wings trying to cool itself. If this is unsuccessful and the heat does not abate, the bird may lose consciousness and even die. If you notice that he is becoming overheated, remove him immediately to a cooler place and run a fan near his cage. Lightly mist him with cool water and offer drops of cool water in his mouth.

Attention!

Just like humans, birds can suffer from stress. Parrotlets are very intelligent and social creatures, so it's important to provide spacious living quarters and plenty of activities to keep your bird from feeling bored and restless, especially if you keep only one bird. Also be prepared to devote time to interact and play with your pet each day; out-of-cage time and attention are necessary for his overall well-being. Birds that are confined, lonely, or kept in stressful situations may pick at themselves or develop other behavior problems attempting to relieve discomfort or frustration. You must be diligent not only in providing general care for your parrotlet but also in making sure he is happy as well.

Your Parrotlet's First Aid Kit

Here is a list of essential items for an avian first aid kit. Keep these items in a small tackle box for convenient access when you need them.

- antibiotic ointment (for small wounds, use a nongreasy product only because oil prevents a bird from keeping in body heat)
- alcohol (for sterilizing tools)
- baby bird formula (can be used for adults having a difficult time eating)
- bag or can of your bird's base diet (in case of evacuation)
- bandages and gauze
- bottled water (you may need clean fresh water to flush out a wound or clean your bird of debris)
- cornstarch (to stop bleeding on the skin or beak)
- cotton balls
- cotton swabs
- dishwashing detergent (mild, for cleaning oil off feathers)
- electrolyte solution for human babies (for reviving a weak bird)
- eyewash
- heating pad (always allow your bird the option of moving off the heating pad)
- hydrogen peroxide (always use in a weak solution with water)
- nail clippers
- nail file
- needle-nosed pliers (for broken blood feathers)
- penlight
- saline solution
- sanitary wipes
- sharp scissors
- small transport cage
- small clean towels (for holding or swabbing)
- spray bottle (for misting)
- styptic powder (to stop bleeding of the nails)
- syringe (without needle)
- tweezers
- veterinarian's phone number and info

Never set a parrotlet's cage out in the sun unless he has a shady spot to retreat to, and never leave a parrotlet in a closed car on a warm day, because birds are easily overcome by heat.

Musculoskeletal System

Birds are fantastic athletes, able to fly for miles a day; as a result, they tend to be well muscled. Parrotlets that have their wings clipped are less well muscled than fully flighted

Quarantine

Quarantine is traditionally a period of 40 days in which a new bird is kept separate from other pets already established in the household. Some people choose to shorten this period to 30 days and find little harm in doing that. During the quarantine period, you'll watch the new bird for signs of illness. You should feed and water him after you care for your other birds, and change your clothing and disinfect your hands after any contact with the bird or the cage. Quarantine is the only way to prevent a new bird from passing a potential illness to the birds you already have. It is sometimes not possible to completely separate a new bird from established birds, but you should try to do your best to keep contact at a minimum while he is being quarantined.

parrotlets. The latter have more "red" than "white" muscles because they are active flying birds, as opposed to grounded birds, such as chickens and turkeys, which don't need as many fat-burning muscles. Many of your parrotlet's bones are filled with air, and all of them are thin-walled, which makes the bird light, a necessary development for flight. A heavy bird expends a lot more energy in the air. While bird bones are strong enough to allow the movement of wings in flight, they are easily broken. If you suspect that one of your parrotlet's bones is broken, take it to the veterinarian immediately. Some of the bones contain air sacs that aid in breathing, further complicating matters should a bone be broken.

Digestive System

The parrotlet's digestive system begins with the beak and ends with the vent. After food is swallowed it goes to the crop, which is near the bird's breast. After going to the crop, the food goes to the stomach (proventriculus), then on to the gizzard (ventriculus), which grinds the food, then on to the cloaca, the place where the feces and urates collect before being eliminated through the vent.

Common Illnesses

Now that you know a little bit about the parrotlet's body and physiology, here are a few diseases and conditions common to these parrots.

Mites

Scaly-face mites, or *Knemidokoptes*, occur in young birds and also in older birds with compromised immune systems. Parakeets (budgies) are the most prone to these kinds of mites, but they are worth mentioning here just in case. These mites cause a crusty appearance on the bird's face and legs and can result in an overgrown beak. They are easy to treat but require multiple treatments. Scaly-face mites are not very contagious but can be passed from bird to bird.

The tiny feather mite is not common in parrotlets, but it can infest birds that live outdoors in unclean conditions. Red mites eat their host's blood and are highly contagious, though not very common in parrotlets. Air sac mites occur more commonly in finches and canaries but can occur in parrotlets and cause a clicking sound when the bird breathes, eventually cutting off the air supply. If you suspect mites, do not try to get rid of them yourself; contact your avian veterinarian.

Giardia

Protozoans of the genus *Giardia* can affect your parrotlet and can also affect other animals in the house, even yourself, and result in the condition known as giardiasis. It is passed by contaminated food or water and affects the digestive tract. You may notice diarrhea, itching, inability to digest foods, weight loss, and other symptoms. Have your veterinarian test for this parasite if your bird shows those signs.

Worms

Roundworms are commonly found in parrotlets and should be tested for on your first veterinary visit. If roundworms are found, routine treatments should be performed on the bird,

usually in the form of oral antiparasitic drugs. Eliminating these worms can sometimes take years.

Aspergillosis

Aspergillosis is a fungal infection that causes respiratory distress and can be deadly. Any changes in your parrotlet's breathing, such as gasping or wheezing, or changes in vocalization, can indicate this infection. Aspergillosis is diagnosable by your avian veterinarian, but it's

Never let your cat and your parrotlet interact. The bacteria on a cat's claws are deadly to most birds.

difficult to treat and may take months of medication and treatment to cure. Prevent this infection by keeping your parrotlet's environment very clean and dry to prevent the growth of mold.

Yeast

Yeast infections, or candidiasis, affect the mouth, digestive tract, and possibly the respiratory system. Your parrotlet normally has a certain amount of yeast in his body, but when his bodily balance is out of whack, as when it's undernourished or after a treatment of antibiotics, the fungus can grow to excess.

A parrotlet with a yeast infection will have a sticky substance in its mouth and may have white mouth lesions. Regurgitation and digestive problems may occur. Treatment by a veterinarian is necessary. Even though this condition is not immediately serious, it can cause death if left untreated. Offering your parrotlet foods that are loaded with vitamin A, such as green leafy vegetables and orange fruits and vegetables, can help prevent yeast infections. Clean housing is also important in keeping yeast at bay.

Tuberculosis

Mycobacterium avium is responsible for the tuberculosis infection in birds and can be transmitted in food or in water or by filthy cage parts. Avian tuberculosis can be transmitted to humans who have compromised immune systems, so the caretaker must be careful to avoid infection. While TB in humans is a respiratory disease, it is primarily a digestive disorder in parrotlets. Symptoms in birds include weight loss and other digestive disorders.

Psittacosis (Parrot Fever)

Psittacosis, also called chlamydiosis and parrot fever, is also transmittable to humans and causes respiratory distress symptoms in both humans and birds. Psittacosis is transmitted through droppings and infected secretions. Some parrotlets can be carriers of the disease without showing any symptoms. Ask your veterinarian to test for this disease, especially if there's someone with a weakened

Signs of Illness

Any of these conditions require an emergency trip to the veterinarian:

broken bones

eye injuries

gasping for air

head trauma

lameness

loss of consciousness

loss of limbs

seizures

severe bleeding

vomiting (with debris sticking to the feathers)

Polyomavirus is usually seen in young birds, although adults can be carriers.

immune system, an elderly person, or an infant in contact with your parrotlet. It is doubtful that you or your parrotlet will come into contact with this illness, but it's important to know about it anyway.

Megabacteria

Megabacteria, also called gastric yeast, is a fungus found in parts of a bird's digestive system. It can cause extreme weight loss and loss of appetite, and diagnosis generally occurs after death, although the disease is treatable if detected. It is not certain whether this fungus actually causes the condition or whether a weakened system and poor nutrition allows it to thrive.

Pasteurella

Bacteria of the genus *Pasteurella* cause a fatal infection in birds; the condition is primarily transmitted through contact with cats, usually through a scratch or a bite, but it may also be transmitted if a bird plays with a cat's toys. These bacteria also occur on rabbits and other small animals, and the disease they cause is lethal for birds. Immediate treatment with strong antibiotics is necessary if your

Importance of Exercise

Although healthy parrotlets are active birds in general, they can become obese if they are overfed or if they don't get enough exercise. Providing spacious living quarters and providing ample out-of-cage time daily can help to prevent this problem. The best exercise is to allow your parrotlet to have free flight inside a large aviary. He can get good exercise playing with you as well. The more exercise your parrotlet gets, the healthier and happier he will be.

parrotlet is bitten or scratched by a cat or a dog. Note that humans can also be affected by these bacteria but that dogs and cats are not.

Psittacine Beak and Feather Disease (PBFD)
PBFD is an incurable, contagious (to other birds) disease that involves feather loss and beak lesions in the later stages of the disease. Diagnosis is through blood testing, and euthanasia is generally recommended after confirmation. This disease is fatal. Symptoms include feather loss, abnormal feather growth, and a generally ill condition.

Polyomavirus
Polyomavirus usually affects young birds, though adult birds are carriers, transmitting the disease to their young, which die around the time they are fledglings. It occurs mainly among breeding stock in crowded conditions, though households with many birds are susceptible as well, especially if you are going to be adding young birds to the household. There is

no treatment for polyomavirus, so prevention is essential. Make sure to have your avian veterinarian test all of your parrotlets for this disease.

Pacheco's Disease
Pacheco's disease is a viral hepatitis that affects the liver. It is fatal and is mainly diagnosed upon death, which comes rapidly. This is a highly contagious disease and can be transmitted easily when you bring a new bird into your home. Always enforce strict quarantine. Pacheco's disease is not commonly found in parrotlets, but it does occur in many other South American species of birds.

Reproductive Disorders
Female parrotlets are prone to extreme egg laying. They will lay eggs without a male present and will continue to lay eggs until something stops them, like a change in environment or death. Most companion birds are triggered to lay eggs in the spring, when the light hours are more than the hours of darkness. If this is the case, you can help alleviate some of that "spring

fever" in your parrotlet by pulling the shades and covering the cage after the bird has gotten nine or ten hours of light. After a while her hormones should subside and she won't lay eggs any more—we hope! A hen that's allowed to lay dozens of eggs a year will have a greatly diminished lifespan.

An undernourished egg-laying hen, especially one that hasn't gotten enough calcium in her diet, may have eggs with soft shells that will be difficult to lay, resulting in egg binding. This can also occur when the egg is malformed or if she has a tumor or other disorder of the reproductive system. Symptoms of egg binding are panting and lameness, among others. Keeping the laying hen fit and nourished will help to prevent egg binding.

Consult your veterinarian immediately if you suspect this problem. If you notice your female bird fluffed and panting on the bottom of her cage, and her belly is distended and her droppings are large and watery, she may be trying to lay an egg. Give her some time to lay it on her own, but if 24 hours pass and she hasn't laid it, you may need to intervene. If you can't get her to an avian veterinarian right away, place one drop of olive oil in her vent (just at the outside of it) and one drop in her mouth. Be careful that you don't choke her—put the drop just on the side of her beak rather than directly into it. This may help to lubricate the area and ease the egg out. If that doesn't work, try it again and move her into a very warm hospital cage and call your avian veterinarian. Even if the bird passes the egg, she might need an examination so that the situation doesn't occur again.

If you keep male and female parrotlets together, they are likely to breed whether you want them to or not.

Older male parrotlets may develop tumors on their testicles (located inside the body), and as a result their ceres may change colors. Regular veterinary checkups should help to find and treat any developing problems such as this one.

Gout

Gout is a painful condition of the legs common in birds that don't get proper nutrition, including lots of fruits and vegetables. Symptoms include visible swellings on the legs and subsequent lameness.

Bumblefoot

Bumblefoot is an infection of the bottom of the feet and is associated with poor nutrition, obesity, lack of adequate perches, perching for too long, and filthy perches. The skin on the bottom of the foot may be inflamed and red and may become scabby, resulting in lameness.

Lameness, foot infections, and other similar problems can be caused by inadequate perches, especially if they are too big for your parrotlet.

Scrambled Eggs

On the topic of eggs, something of interest that's unique to parrotlets – their eggs are proportionately huge in comparison to their bodies. When you see parrotlet eggs next to the hen that laid them, it's almost inconceivable that they could have come from her! Hens generally lay an average of about six eggs. If they eggs are fertile, they hatch in about 19 days, each egg hatching about a day apart. The babies fledge (leave the nest) in about five weeks, but they keep returning to the nest to be fed by the parents for about eight weeks, at which time the parents will wean them onto adult food.

Birds and Bees

The birds and the bees...you can't stop them. But you can prevent your birds from having unwanted babies should they begin mating. First, do not provide them with anything resembling a nest. If they lay eggs in the feed dishes, remove the dishes and replace them with smaller dishes. If they lay eggs on the floor of the cage, simply remove them and throw them away. If the egg laying persists, cut back on the light that your birds get to about 10 hours a day. More than 12 hours of light can cause the birds' hormones to spike, causing them to want to breed.

Lameness

Lameness and weakness in the feet are sometimes associated with egg-bound hens, but there can be multiple reasons for it, including tumors. See your avian veterinarian if you notice any foot or leg weakness.

Senior Bird Care

Because parrotlets can live to be 20 years old or more, they aren't considered "senior" until they are about 15. Unfortunately, because proper bird care is actually quite difficult, their life span is often reduced by a third.

A very elderly bird might have trouble getting around and may need his perches lowered and his food served on the floor of his cage. He might want to sleep on paper towels on the bottom of his cage because his feet may pain him somewhat. If the older bird lives with other younger birds, keep an eye on him so that they don't pick on him if he becomes infirm or ill. Watch his general condition so that you can catch any health problems early.

6

Training
Your
Parrotlet

Part of the fun of living with a parrotlet is being able to have physical contact with him. Untamed birds may bite and try to flee when you attempt to handle them simply because they aren't used to that kind of attention. They aren't misbehaving—they just haven't learned yet that you aren't going to harm them. When most people think of "training" their parrotlet, what they really mean is *taming*. Training involves an end result behavior and a learning process. Taming is simply socialization to different stimuli. You will discover how to do both in this chapter.

Parrotlets can *in theory* be trained to perform simple behaviors; however, it's more likely that your bird will train you than the other way around. Parrotlets learn quickly what works to get what they want. If your bird is begging to be let out of his cage with high-pitched whistles and a frantic dance in front of his door, and then you open the cage, he will learn that the behavior works. This is called "positive reinforcement," and it is the basis for effective training.

Positive Reinforcement

Positive reinforcement behavior modification is based on the theory that animals (including humans) will continue to perform a behavior that works to achieve a certain goal, one where a reward is earned. When a behavior doesn't prove to be effective to earn the desired reward, the animal will usually try something different to see whether the new behavior works better. When you reward desired behaviors and ignore unwanted ones, you are reinforcing the desired behavior and making it more likely that it will happen again.
parrot-1

For example, let's say that the bird wants to get out of the cage to play, so he bounces around the door making noise. You let him out because the "dance" is so cute. He will do that

Begin Training Early

Before you begin taming or training your parrotlet, he must be comfortable in his new surroundings, as well as comfortable with you. The key to training a bird—or any other animal—is trust. Once he has adjusted, you can begin to hand-tame him. Beginning early is also essential. Whether you have a young bird or an older one, start training him a week to ten days after bringing him home because the longer you wait, the more difficult it will be. An untamed adult is not a hopeless case, however; the process will just take longer and require more patience. Parrotlets can be stubborn,but may be convinced to be hands-on companions with a lot of gentle positive reinforcement.

dance again to try to get you to let him out again. If it works, the behavior will continue to be reinforced until it doesn't work anymore. If you stop letting him out when he does the dance, the behavior will eventually become extinct and he will try something else. This is the basis for the kind of taming and training that works best with parrotlets.

For taming and training to work, you must first develop a relationship with your parrotlet. Don't force him to do anything he doesn't want to do, and respect him as you would a good friend. A bird that views his guardian as a friend is more likely to become tame. Fear tactics don't work with birds, but gentle, patient training methods do. Speak softly to him and handle him tenderly. Know your parrotlet's limitations before you set out to teach him complicated behaviors, and don't push anything on him before he's ready.

A parrotlet that views his guardian as a friend is much more likely to be tame and sociable.

Socialization

Socialization is the process by which you introduce your bird to everything he will encounter in the household or outside. If you do this while he's young he will grow up unafraid of the objects of everyday life. An older bird that has not been socialized to household items will fear them, and he may not ever get used to things like the vacuum cleaner, household pets, or strangers. However, parrotlets are much less wary of these things than some larger species and are pretty easy-going about items that are new to the environment.

To socialize the bird to odd objects, like the vacuum cleaner, begin by placing the object across the room from the bird's cage. Or, if the item is

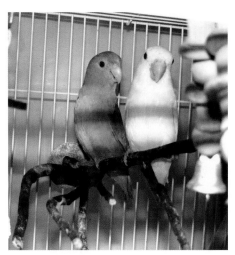

It's important that your parrotlets are carefully socialized to each other before you try housing them together.

eventually to be inside the parrotlet's cage, like a new perch that he might be scared of, place it on a table just a few feet from the cage where he can easily see it. Every two to three days, move the object a little closer to the cage. Don't rush. Allow the bird to begin to accept the item in his environment. In the case of the vacuum cleaner or other noise-making objects, you will have to move the item closer until it's right next to the cage for a few days, but then start back at stage one when you're going to begin turning it on. Most parrotlets don't have issues with many household objects, so you won't have to do much of this.

Other pets, especially dogs, cats, and other predators, can be scary for a new bird. Eventually the bird will get used to the presence of these other animals. Make sure that his cage is very secure and that the other pets can't get into it or knock it over. Don't try to do face-to-face introductions with dogs and cats. To them, the parrotlet probably looks like a fun toy or treat. Parrotlets are in grave danger with cats around, so take extreme precaution that cats can't get anywhere near the birdcage. Cats and dogs have *Pasteurella* bacteria in their mouths and claws, which is deadly to birds.

Introducing the bird to the human members of the family is easier. Don't pull the bird out on the first day home and pass him around. He has to get used to his new housing, environment, other pets, and new people. If he's alone, he probably isn't used to being without other birds. Play the radio or TV for him so that he has some noise in his environment—he's used to that from the pet store or breeder. Parrotlets don't like dead silence during the day.

After a couple of days, have everyone begin approaching the cage and speaking softly or singing to the bird. After a few more days, people can begin offering millet spray through the bars and encouraging the bird to take a few nibbles. The idea is to do this very slowly so that the bird engages with everyone in a positive manner; if someone scares him, his taming will be set back.

Taming

A very young parrotlet is easy to

Carrier Training

Most parrotlets will acclimate easily to a travel carrier and don't need a lot of socialization with it. Simply put it near the cage and include it in playtime, putting the bird inside and then taking him right out again. Put some toys in and on top of the carrier, and allow him to play there. When you travel, include some millet spray, seed, and a very shallow dish of water. A water bottle is recommended, but if your parrotlet isn't used to drinking from one, he may not know how and will dehydrate, so use a coop cup instead and put in only a little bit of water so that it doesn't spill everywhere. Put paper towels on the bottom of the carrier so that the bird has good footing. Don't include a perch, but you can include a rolled-up washcloth for the bird to stand on.

handle because he's far less likely to bite and is more likely to be gentle and willing to try new things. Handle your youngster every day starting with the day after you bring him home. Have him stand in the palm of your hand or on your finger. Don't press him to do more than he's prepared to do. For example, this isn't the time to train him to stay on a play gym. Instead, sit on the floor in a safe room and have him perch on your shoulder, a very secure area, or on your finger with your hand close to your chest. Talk and whistle to him. Put him back after about ten minutes, and repeat several times a day. Make these handling sessions relaxing and fun for him. If he becomes stressed when you're handling him, he won't want to come out of the cage for you, and he'll begin to use his only two modes of defense, fight (biting) and flight (flapping around the cage).

A semi-tame parrotlet may have been handled before but also may be mistrustful of humans.

If you acquired a hand-raised parrotlet, he will likely be tame right from the start.

Flown the Coop?

Prevent the loss of your parrotlet by adding screens to your windows and making sure he's caged before opening any doors. Never take him outside unless you're positive that he has a very good wing clip, or he's in a safe carrier. If you do lose your bird, hunt for him outside, and calling his name. Tell all of your neighbors and make up posters offering a reward. Call all of the vets and animal shelters in the area. If he has a friend (another parrotlet), take the bird outside in a cage and encourage the bird to chirp, which may bring your wayward parrotlet down from a tree. Finally, cross your fingers.

The main problem with the semi-tame bird is that he's not tame enough to have meaningful interactions with you yet, but he's tame enough to get near your hand to bite it. But you can tame this bird easily if you take some simple steps toward developing a trusting relationship with him.

There are two basic ways to tame a parrotlet, similar to how you'd train a horse. You can "break" him or you can "gentle" him. Using a gentle, slow training method is always preferable with almost any animal but especially with an animal as sensitive as a parrot. "Breaking" a parrotlet using quick, forceful training will work for a time but does not allow a real bond to form.

Give your semi-tame parrotlet a period of adjustment when you first bring him home. He will be stressed in his new situation. Do not consider taming him until he has settled into a routine. This may take a few days to more than a week. Once a parrotlet is eating well, vocalizing, preening, and bathing, he is adjusted to his new home and you can begin with short taming sessions.

Once your new bird is settled in, you will first need to clip his wings if they aren't clipped already. A parrotlet with free flight will fly away from you and not return for the taming session! Even if you want to allow your bird to fly eventually, you will have to clip the wings during the training period; the feathers will grow back in time.

Remove your bird from his cage with a small washcloth and hold him gently to prevent him from biting you. He may scream and struggle, but be calm and talk to him in a soothing voice. Take him to a small, safe room— the bathroom is ideal—but close the toilet lid and remove any dangerous items that may fall and break if he comes in contact with them. Ideally, the room should be somewhat dimly lit, but not dark.

Sit on the floor with your knees bent into "mountains" in front of you, then place the bird gently on top of one of your knees, holding him there for a moment before you let go. The minute you let go, the bird will probably flutter away from you. Gather up the bird and try to place him on your knee again. Repeat this action until he eventually stands for a moment on your knee. He may not want to stay there in the first few sessions, but keep trying. Do this two or three times a day for 10 to 20 minutes each session, but no more than that.

Training and taming your parrotlet requires patience and kindness.

Once you've gotten your bird to stand on your knee, talk to him in a very calm voice and begin to move one hand slowly up your leg toward him. Little by little, session after session, move your hand slowly up your leg until the bird allows it to

Be Patient!

You can't tame a frightened or ill bird. Your parrotlet will be best tamed when he is content and relaxed. Signs of a happy and calm bird are: preening and grooming, fluffing feathers, yawning, being playful, and showing a lot of interest in what you're doing. Most importantly, never yell at or punish your parrotlet—it won't work and will damage any trust that you have established. Be patient, keep training sessions short, and have realistic expectations.

come very close. The idea here is that he should eventually allow contact with your hand. This may take quite a while, so be patient. Once the bird allows your hand to approach closely, try to tickle his chest with your finger or scratch his head and neck if he allows, still moving very slowly. If he is particularly skittish, move a millet spray up your leg toward him before you offer your hand. It's a great sign if he nibbles on the spray. After a few sessions, you can begin to try to get the bird to stand on your hand.

At the end of the training session, place your parrotlet back in his cage. If you have trouble with that, put your hand gently over the bird's back so he can't open his wings to try to fly away or attempt to climb on the outside of the cage.

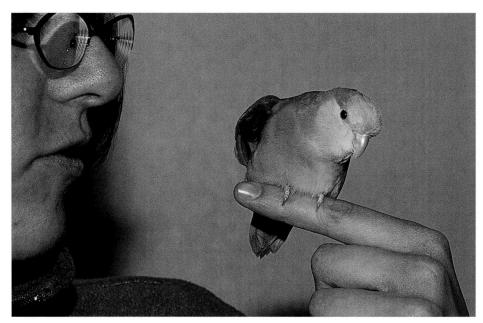

It is important to teach your parrotlet to step up. This allows you to retrieve him whenever you need to do so.

An untamed parrotlet is one that has not had much, if any, handling by humans. He is fearful of humans and can be aggressive, but he's not impossible to tame. After letting him adjust to his new home, you have to show him that you aren't afraid of him. If you are bitten and you retreat, you show him that he has an effective tool for making you go away. The best way to deal with biting is to avoid being bitten. This means that you may want to work with stick training before you begin using your hands (you'll get directions for stick training later in the chapter). Don't use gloves—you want the bird to become used to hands, and using gloves defeats that.

If your parrotlet is extremely untamed, you can hold him properly and gently in a towel and talk softly to him while caressing his head. Do this twice a day for the first few days before you begin training him. Your parrotlet does not like to be restrained like this, but he will come to understand that you aren't hurting him, even though being restrained is uncomfortable. Use this method *only* if you are certain that holding your parrotlet is not causing him pain or undue stress, and do it for only a few minutes at a time.

Step-Up and Stick Training
Of all the behaviors you can teach

your parrotlet, *step-up* is the most important. This behavior allows you to retrieve your parrotlet at any time and is especially useful when he's in danger. Step-up is when your parrotlet steps gently onto your hand or finger without hesitating. It's important to reinforce this command so that it becomes second nature to your bird. If he's used to standing on your finger or a stick, he's more likely to do it when you require. Fortunately, this behavior comes very naturally to parrots, so teaching it to a tame bird is a breeze.

Training Step-Up
Assuming that you're teaching a tame or semi-tame parrotlet the step-up behavior, begin by allowing him to come out of his cage on his own. If he will step onto your hand, bring him out that way—you're on the right track to reinforcing this behavior. Place a perch on top of his cage, or place him onto a play gym where he will be standing on a round dowel, not a flat surface.

Give him a treat like millet spray. Next, begin rubbing your bird's chest and belly very softly and gently with the length of your index finger, talking to him soothingly, slowly increasing the pressure with which you push on his chest. If he steps onto your hand, praise him and then put him back on the perch and repeat. If he doesn't step up, you can increase the pressure. Pushing slightly on a parrotlet's chest throws him off balance, so he will lift up a foot to right himself. Place your finger or hand under the foot and lift him, if he allows it. If not, simply

Don't Do List

There are a few things you should never do during training. Do not "punish" or discipline a parrotlet—it will only ruin the bond of trust between you if you do. Here's a list of parrotlet "nevers":

- Never hit, flick, squeeze, or throw your parrotlet. This is animal abuse.

- Never hold or flick the beak. It is very sensitive!

- Never throw anything at your parrotlet's cage to make him stop vocalizing. This will make him feel very insecure.

- Never "play rough."

- Never cover the cage for long periods during the day. If you have a sleeping infant or you need your bird to quiet down, cover it for an hour or so. It's cruel to cover the cage for extended periods when your parrotlet should be active.

- Never starve your parrotlet as a training tool. He has a fast metabolism and can die if prevented from eating for a day or two.

Rewards Get Results

You might need to give your parrotlet a little more motivation during taming or training sessions, so try to find a food that your parrotlet will do anything to get. Most are very attracted to millet spray. As you get to know your bird, you'll discover what he likes. The ideal treat is anything he will rush to get. You will give him just a taste, then pull the treat away until the next time he does something right. Reward desired behaviors as much as possible for the best results. Don't be stingy with praise or treats!

allow his foot to remain on your hand until he removes it. As you do this, tell your bird clearly to step up. Always say "step up" when he steps onto your hand so that he comes to associate the behavior with the words.

Once your parrotlet is fairly good at stepping up, have him step from finger to finger, repeating the phrase "step up," and praising/rewarding him when he performs. He may hesitate at first, but soon he'll know exactly what you want. Be sure that your training sessions last only a few minutes each, and incorporate them into playtime. Try not to become frustrated if your parrotlet doesn't do exactly what you want right away. Most youngsters will learn the step-up behavior easily, in one or two short sessions, though a semi-tame parrotlet may take longer. The more your bird trusts you, the easier it is to teach him anything. Even if the step-up behavior is the only "trick" you teach him, is it by far the most valuable.

Stick Training
Stick training is simply teaching the

step-up behavior using a perch or dowel instead of your finger. It's critical that your parrotlet know how to step onto a stick. The day may come when he refuses to come down from the curtain rod, or gets out of the house and is sitting in the branches of a tree. A parrotlet that has been stick trained will be easier to retrieve with a long dowel or broomstick. One that isn't used to stepping onto a stick will be terrified of it, and, as a result, you may lose the opportunity to save your bird.

Teach the bird to step up using a stick the same way you teach it with your finger. Stick training should begin as soon as you begin hand-taming your parrotlet. If your bird is terrified of the stick, leave it close to the cage where he will have a chance to view it and get used to its presence. Move it closer and closer, and eventually put it on top of the cage, and then into the cage before training with it. Allow the bird to live with it for awhile. Use different types of sticks during training, so that your parrotlet is comfortable with various dowels and perches, but don't use a slick dowel or he might fall off, making him afraid of these kinds of perches in the future.

"Whittle-Down" Training Method

Being afraid of your parrotlet's beak is understandable. The bite isn't terribly painful, but it can hurt. If you want to avoid being bitten, try the "whittle-down" taming method. Begin by stick training your bird with the step-up command using a 12- to 18-inch (30.5- to 45.7-cm) dowel or perch that's an appropriately sized width for a parrotlet. Once your bird learns to step onto the stick and does it with ease, begin cutting the stick shorter, about an inch each week, until the stick is very short. Eventually, if you've done this slowly enough and have worked to gain your bird's trust, the stick will be so short that he will naturally step onto your hand.

Talking

Parrotlets are not the best talkers in the parrot family, but they are able to learn a few words and phrases—probably between five and fifteen, perhaps fewer. They don't speak as clearly as the larger parrots that are good talkers either. The similarly sized budgie is also a much better talker than the parrotlets. Teaching your parrotlet to talk can take some time. Some gifted parrotlets will learn to talk in just a few weeks, and others may not talk for a year, or ever. Repetition, repetition, repetition—that's just about all you need to know to

Parrotlets are not reliable talkers. Some will learn a few words and others won't.

teach any bird to talk.

Your parrotlet's first attempts at talking will sound garbled. Once this "baby talk" begins, you'll start to hear words becoming clearer. This is the time to correct your bird's pronunciation, repeating the phrases that he's attempting (if you understand them) the way they should sound. You'll be surprised at how clearly your parrotlet will begin to repeat words if you teach him how they're meant to be pronounced.

Pairs are less likely to talk than the single bird, and single birds with mirrors are often less likely to talk than single birds without mirrors. If a parrotlet has something to talk to, he won't likely talk to you. But it's sad to force a bird to be lonely so that he'll talk, so you may need a compromise. Wait until your bird learns to talk, and *then* get him a friend or mirror toy to pal around with.

Learning to talk is a parrotlet's way of attempting to communicate with the rest of the household. Talking indicates a deep affection for his guardians, or at least a heightened attentiveness. The more attention and affection you lavish on your bird, the more likely he is to talk to you.

Male parrotlets speak with more frequency and will learn more words than females. There are exceptions, of course, but this is the general rule. Females do become capable whistlers, however, so don't worry—they will mimic sounds they hear. If you really want your parrotlet to talk, don't teach him to whistle first. Whistling is easier and more fun, apparently, than talking. You can teach your bird to whistle after he has learned several phrases. Of course, if you have a female, you can teach whistling from the beginning.

The only way to teach your bird to talk is to repeat yourself a lot. A parrotlet has to hear a word or phrase many times before he masters it. Most birds learn things their guardians say to them every day, such as their name, "good morning," "good night," "pretty bird," "Want some food?," and so on. Once you've decided on a phrase you want your parrotlet to learn, say it over and over every time you pass the cage, and be sure to say it clearly so that he will hear it correctly. Words with hard sounds like p, t, c, k, b, and d are easiest to learn.

Kids and Training

Children, in particular, must be trained to handle a parrotlet gently and with composure. Always supervise young children while they are handling birds, especially during training. Though a parrotlet's bite may not hurt an adult much, it can definitely break the skin of a child's hand. Make sure the bird is tame before training sessions begin. Youngsters can offer treats and sing to calm the bird. Teach them not to move quickly or make fast hand motions while doing so.

Tricks

Parrotlets can be taught simple tricks, but they are not known to be proficient at learning intricate behaviors. The best way to teach tricks is to capitalize on natural behaviors and reward the ones you like. For example, if you notice that your parrotlet is great at climbing, place him on the end of a long piece of rope and encourage him to climb up, praising him in a high-pitched voice when he completes the task—placing a millet spray at the top of the rope doesn't hurt. If he jumps off before he reaches the top, start again, this time

Praise and reward your parrotlet often to keep training fun for him.

encouraging him and praising when he's climbing and stopping when he jumps off. Remember, whenever you want to teach your parrotlet anything, use a lot of praise and make the training session fun. Also, if you can find a treat that your parrotlet adores, millet spray, for example, use it in your training sessions rather than just offering it freely in the cage.

Problem Behaviors

Though there aren't "problem parrotlets," there are problem behaviors that you can resolve either through behavior modification, boosting the bird's health, or changing the way the bird lives in order to make the behavior cease. Let's look closely at a few behaviors that guardians often complain about.

Biting

Biting occurs when a bird is fearful and feeling cornered. He doesn't want the type of attention you're offering. Parrotlets also bite when they're protecting their cage, mate, or nest. If your feathered friend tries to bite you, consider what's going on at the time. Are you trying to handle an untamed bird? Are you trying to pick up a bird that's protecting eggs? Begin with the basics of socialization and taming to resolve the problem.

If a previously tame bird starts biting, he may have a health issue or is becoming hormonal, or perhaps the bird has been left alone so long that he has reverted in his training. Maybe something has traumatized him and he no longer wants a human hand near him. Try to see it from his point of view. If you determine that he's healthy, you can potentially get him to stop biting by moving his cage, or moving around the toys and perches inside the cage. Sometimes a little change of scenery helps. For playtime, remove the bird from the room where his cage is, and try handling him in a safe place that he's not all that familiar with.

Screaming

Parrotlets chitter-chatter for much of the day, and there's not much you're going to be able to do about it. They are not notorious screamers and generally don't annoy the household or the neighbors. If you hear genuine screaming from your parrotlet, he might have his toe or head caught in a toy, or perhaps he has injured himself or something is scaring him.

Chewing

Parrotlets love to chew, especially on soft wood and paper. Chewing generally isn't a problem as long as you give your bird safe toys to chew on. If you allow your parrotlet out inside your home, watch him carefully to make sure he doesn't get into anything he can bite on, such as houseplants, picture frames, and so on. You're not going to prevent him from chewing; you can only prevent him from getting to the items he wants to chew but you don't want him to.

Body Language

Here are a few things to look out for with your parrotlet's body language:

Sleeping posture: a healthy parrotlet will sleep on one foot, with the other tucked into his belly; his head will be either tucked into his neck or turned around and resting on his back.

Wing flapping: also called wing drumming, this is when a bird stands on his perch and flaps his wings wildly, a sign he is content or is communicating with you.

Regurgitating: a high compliment, this happens when birds feed one another or their chicks regurgitated food; birds that are very affectionate with their humans may also do this with a person, or with a favored toy.

Beak grinding: you may hear your bird make a little grinding noise with his beak before he falls asleep; this is a sign of comfort and contentment.

This parrotlet has his head down and feathers raised, indicating excitement or even aggression.

Feather Plucking

A parrotlet that's plucking his feathers out or is chewing them and becoming scruffy and fluffy looking has a serious problem. Like other parrots, parrotlets can begin feather mutilation due to boredom, but this behavior is more likely due to illness or a skin condition. See a veterinarian immediately if you notice bald patches or fluffy patches; a healthy molting bird will lose feathers gradually all over his body, not in patches. See Chapter 4 for more information on feather plucking.

Resources

Organizations

American Federation of Aviculture
P.O.Box 7312
N. Kansas City, MO 64116
Telephone: (816) 421-3214
Fax: (816)421-3214
E-mail: afaoffice@aol.com
www.afabirds.org

Avicultural Society of America
PO Box 5516
Riverside, CA 92517-5516
Telephone: (951) 780-4102
Fax: (951) 789-9366
E-mail: info@asabirds.org
www.asabirds.org

Aviculture Society of the United
Kingdom
Arcadia-The Mounts-East Allington-
Totnes
Devon TQ9 7QJ
United Kingdom
E-mail: admin@avisoc.co.uk
www.avisoc.co.uk/

The Gabriel Foundation
1025 Acoma Street
Denver, CO 80204
Telephone: (970) 963-2620
Fax: (970) 963-2218
E-mail: gabriel@thegabrielfoundation.
org
www.thegabrielfoundation.org

International Association of Avian
Trainers and Educators
350 St. Andrews Fairway
Memphis, TN 38111
Telephone: (901) 685-9122
Fax: (901) 685-7233
E-mail: secretary@iaate.org
www.iaate.org

International Parrotlet Society
PO Box 2428
Santa Cruz, CA 95063-2428
Telephone: (831)688-5560
Fax: (831) 689-9534
www.internationalparrotletsociety.org

The Parrot Society of Australia
P.O. Box 75
Salisbury, Queensland 4107
Australia
E-mail: petbird@parrotsociety.org.au
http: //www.partosociety.org.au

Emergency Resources and Rescue Organizations

ASPCA Animal Poison Control
Center
Telephone: (888) 426-4435
E-mail: napcc@aspca.org (for non-
emergency, general information only)
www.apcc.aspca.org

Bird Hotline
P.O. Box 1411
Sedona, AZ 86339-1411
E-mail: birdhotline@birdhotline.com
www.birdhotline.com/

Bird Placement Program
P.O. Box 347392
Parma, OH 44134
Telephone: (330) 722-1627
E-mail: birdrescue5@hotmail.com
www.birdrescue.com

Parrot Rehabilitation Society
P.O. Box 620213
San Diego, CA 92102
Telephone: (619) 224-6712
E-mail: prsorg@yahoo.com
www.parrotsociety.org

Petfinder
www.petfinder.com

Veterinary Resources

Association of Avian Veterinarians
P.O.Box 811720
Boca Raton, FL 33481-1720
Telephone: (561) 393-8901
Fax: (561) 393-8902
E-mail: AAVCTRLOFC@aol.com
www.aav.org

Exotic Pet Vet.Net
www.exoticpetvet.net

Internet Resources

AvianWeb
http://www.avianweb.com/

BirdCLICK
www.geocities.com/Heartland/
Acres/9154/

Forpus.com
www.parrotlets.com/forpus/

HolisticBird.org
www.holisticbird.org

The Parrot Pages
www.parrotpages.com

Parrot Parrot
www.parrotparrot.com/

Parrotlet Express Yahoo Group
pets.groups.yahoo.com/group/
ParrotletExpress/

Parrotlet Species Identification
shadypines.com/plets.htm

Parrotlets.us
www.parrotlets.us

ParrotletsPlus Yahoo Group
pets.groups.yahoo.com/group/
ParrotletsPlus/

Talk Parrotlets
talkparrotlets.com/

Magazines

Bird Talk
3 Burroughs
Irvine, CA 92618
Telephone: 949-855-8822
Fax: (949) 855-3045
www.birdtalkmagazine.com

Good Bird
PO Box 684394
Austin, TX 78768
Telephone: 512-423-7734
Fax: (512) 236-0531
E-mail: info@goodbirdinc.com
www.goodbirdinc.com

Books

Deutsch, Robin. *Good Parrotkeeping.* TFH Publications, Inc.

Deutsch, Robin. *The Click That Does the Trick.* TFH Publications, Inc.

Deutsch, Robin. *The Healthy Bird Cookbook.* TFH Publications, Inc.

Heidenreich, Barbara. *The Parrot Problem Solver.* TFH Publications, Inc.

Moutsaki, Nikki. *Your Outta Control Bird.* TFH Publications, Inc.

O'Connor, Rebecca K. *A Parrot for Life.* TFH Publications, Inc.

Index

Boldfaced numbers indicate illustrations.

About the Author

Nikki Moustaki is an avian care and behavior expert and consultant with a focus on parrots. She has authored numerous books and magazine articles on bird care and training and has also been featured on television and radio shows for her pet expertise. She hosts the website www.goodbird.com.

Photo Credits

Larry Allan: 65
Joan Balzarini: 1, 3, 12, 17, 18, 32, 40, 42, 47, 49, 50, 54, 56, 66, 71, 72, 76, 85, 86, 87, 91, 95, 96, 99, 101, 103
Sara Bossert (from Shutterstock): 36
Cuson (from Shutterstock): 31
Getideaka (from Shutterstock): 67
Kevin H. Knuth (from Shutterstock): cover
Steve Letter: 9, 11, 46, 70
Rich Lindie (from Shutterstock): 8
Julie Mancini: 29
Nito (from Shutterstock): 43
Linda Ott: 83, 92, 93
Aspen Rock (from Shutterstock): 45
Jean Schweitzer (from Shutterstock): 81
Ronald R. Smith: 55
Laura Steff: 22, 24, 63
John Tyson: 37
Martha White: 6, 28, 58, 60

We Are...

Super Pet®

Everything you need for your Super Pet!

Super Pet is a family of pet lovers working together to bring you fun, functional and quality products that address the needs of both you and your pet bird. We provide everything from cages to toys and accessories all designed to keep your pet bird happy, healthy and safe.